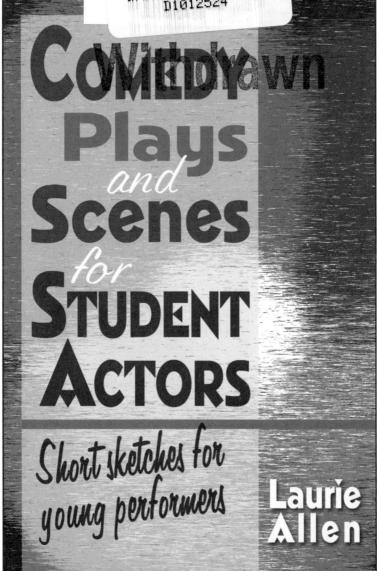

# Comedy Plays and Scenes for Student Actors

## Short sketches for young performers

### Laurie Allen

MERIWETHER PUBLISHING LTD.
Colorado Springs, Colorado

**Meriwether Publishing Ltd., Publisher**
PO Box 7710
Colorado Springs, CO 80933-7710

www.meriwether.com

**Editor: Theodore O. Zapel**
**Assistant editor: Amy Hammelev**
**Cover design: Jan Melvin**

© Copyright MMXI Meriwether Publishing Ltd.
Printed in the United States of America
First Edition

**Library of Congress Cataloging-in-Publication Data**

Allen, Laurie, 1962-
    Comedy plays and scenes for student actors : short sketches for young
performers / by Laurie Allen. -- 1st ed.
        p. cm.
    ISBN 978-1-56608-177-1
    1. Young adult drama, American. 2. Teenagers--Drama. I. Title.
    PS3601.L4324C56 2011
    792.9'5--dc22
                                        2010053685


    1    2    3            11    12    13

*To Chuck*

*for your encouragement and support*

# Table of Contents

# I. Speed Dating

CAST: (5M, 2F) WENDY, SETH, HAROLD, MARTIN,
LIONEL, JENNIFER, BRADLEY
PROPS: Piece of notebook paper, report card, small
notepad, pen
SETTING: Coffee house

1    *(At rise, WENDY sits alone at a table as SETH rushes in and*
2    *sits down across from her. Each time the bell rings, the boys*
3    *must leave and go to another table.)*
4    **SETH: OK, so I have one minute, right?**
5    **WENDY: That's the rule.**
6    **SETH: One minute. One minute! One minute to impress you.**
7    **Does my minute start the minute I sit down or the minute**
8    **we start talking?**
9    **WENDY: The minute you sit down.**
10    **SETH: One minute! One minute! One minute!** *(Pause as he*
11    *struggles)* **Wow. I've never tried this speed dating thing**
12    **before. Have you?**
13    **WENDY: No.**
14    **SETH: Hey, that's something we have in common. We're both**
15    **new to this. Thirty dates in thirty minutes. What more**
16    **could you ask for? Unless of course after thirty dates no**
17    **one liked you. That would be sad. Really sad.**
18    **WENDY: Which is why you should make the most out of the one**
19    **minute you're allowed. So we can see if we make a**
20    **connection.**
21    **SETH: And I've told you nothing about myself, have I? Where do**
22    **I start? Where oh where do I start? Oh, where do I start?**
23    **WENDY: Anywhere would be great.**
24    **SETH: Anywhere. OK, anywhere ... And only one minute to do**
25    **this!**
26    **WENDY: Maybe you'd like to tell me your name?**
27    **SETH: My name. Yes, I should tell you my name. I'm** — *(Bell*
28    *rings.)*

1   WENDY: Time's up.

2   SETH: Time's up?

3   WENDY: You have to move to the next table.

4   SETH: But —

5   WENDY: Bye.

6   SETH: But —

7   HAROLD: *(Enters.)* My turn.

8   WENDY: Bye.

9   SETH: Bye. *(Exits.)*

10  HAROLD: *(Sits down, unfolds a piece of notebook paper, and*
11      *reads dryly.)* Hello. My name is Harold Jewaski. What I
12      would like for you to know about me is that I'm smart,
13      funny, and cute. How, may you ask? If I could submit to
14      you my last report card. *(Hands her a report card.)* As you
15      will see, I made straight As. Now, onto my comedic
16      personality. As you know, most brainiacs such as myself
17      lack sense of humor, but if I may submit to you a joke.
18      Knock knock. *(Silence)* Knock knock. *(Silence)* And you say,
19      "Who's there?"

20  WENDY: Who's there?

21  HAROLD: Apple.

22  WENDY: Apple who?

23  HAROLD: Knock knock.

24  WENDY: Are you starting over?

25  HAROLD: Say, "Who's there?"

26  WENDY: But I already said it.

27  HAROLD: Say it again. Knock knock.

28  WENDY: Who's there?

29  HAORLD: Apple.

30  WENDY: Apple who?

31  HAROLD: Knock knock.

32  WENDY: *(Becoming frustrated)* Who's there?

33  HAROLD: Apple.

34  WENDY: Apple who?

35  HAROLD: Knock knock.

1   WENDY: *Who's there?* Please, just tell me who's there!

2   HAROLD: Orange.

3   WENDY: I thought you said it was apple.

4   HAROLD: Say "Orange who?"

5   WENDY: *(Takes a deep breath.)* Orange who?

6   HAROLD: Orange you glad I didn't say apple? *(He laughs while*

7      *she glares at him. Bell rings.)*

8   WENDY: Time's up.

9   HAROLD: *(Stands, reading.)* Smart, funny, and cute. You're a

10     perfect match. So please pick me. *(Exits.)*

11   MARTIN: *(Enters and sits down.)* Hey.

12   WENDY: Hey.

13   MARTIN: So what's up?

14   WENDY: What's up?

15   MARTIN: Yeah, what's up?

16   WENDY: Not much.

17   MARTIN: Yeah, me neither. *(Pause as he glances around the*

18     *room)* So, this speed dating thing is way up there, isn't it?

19   WENDY: Way up there?

20   MARTIN: Yeah, way up there. You know?

21   WENDY: I guess.

22   MARTIN: So how do you like it so far?

23   WENDY: How do you like it?

24   MARTIN: How do I like it?

25   WENDY: That's what I asked.

26   MARTIN: I like it. That's why I said it was way up there. You

27     know, it rocks.

28   WENDY: Right.

29   MARTIN: So have you found one?

30   WENDY: Found one what?

31   MARTIN: A date.

32   WENDY: Aren't we on one?

33   MARTIN: This is a one-minute introduction, not a date. So,

34     have you found one?

35   WENDY: Not yet.

1   **MARTIN: Me neither. And without trying to hurt your feelings,**
2       **I think I'll just go ahead and move on.**
3   **WENDY: You're leaving early?**
4   **MARTIN: Sorry. Either you connect or you don't.**
5   **WENDY: And we don't?**
6   **MARTIN: I'm not feeling it.**
7   **WENDY: Me neither.** *(Bell rings.)*
8   **MARTIN: See ya.** *(Exits.)*
9   **LIONEL:** *(Enters and sits down.)* **Well, three out of three for me.**
10  **WENDY: Three out of three?**
11  **LIONEL: Three phone numbers.**
12  **WENDY: So, this speed dating is working for you?**
13  **LIONEL:** *(Opens pad of paper and holds pen.)* **Name?**
14  **WENDY: Wendy.**
15  **LIONEL: Phone number?**
16  **WENDY: Aren't we supposed to talk first and see if we're a**
17      **match?**
18  **LIONEL: We can skip that part. All the girls like me. Hey, can I**
19      **get your e-mail address, too?**
20  **WENDY: Uh ... no.**
21  **LIONEL: That way I can send you a schedule.**
22  **WENDY: A schedule of what?**
23  **LIONEL: Of the times that I'm available. So many dates. So**
24      **little time. In fact, I'm starting to stress a bit over this. I**
25      **may have to get a job. A date every night. Inflation. This is**
26      **going to get expensive.**
27  **WENDY: Well, let me help you out here.**
28  **LIONEL: Great! You're offering to pay when we go out? Hey,**
29      **that works for me. And what was your number? Wait.**
30      **What was your name?**
31  **WENDY: Wendy, and I'm not paying.**
32  **LIONEL: Dutch? We each pay our own way? I guess that will be**
33      **OK.** *(Writing)* **Brenda?**
34  **WENDY: Wendy!**
35  **LIONEL:** *(Writes.)* **Wendy. Will pay her own way.** *(To WENDY)*

1      I'm putting a star by your name. Phone number?

2  WENDY: Let's say I not give you my phone number.

3  LIONEL: You're not going to give me your phone number? Why

4      not? Everyone else did. You don't like me?

5  WENDY: I'm offering to take some of the pressure off of you.

6      Because by the end of the night you will have so many

7      dates that you won't know what to do or who to call first.

8  LIONEL: True.

9  WENDY: So let me offer to withhold my phone number so I

10     don't pile any more stress on you.

11  LIONEL: Oh, OK. Thanks. I think.

12  WENDY: No problem. *(Bell rings. LIONEL exits.)*

13  JENNIFER: *(Rushes over and sits down.)* I need a break. I'm

14     sitting here for the next round.

15  WENDY: I need a break, too.

16  JENNIFER: Any luck?

17  WENDY: No. I mean, I've been asked for my phone number, but

18     I didn't give it out. The last guy was so pushy and

19     conceited. I was glad when he left.

20  JENNIFER: Why can't Mr. Right come along and sit down?

21  WENDY: Probably because he's out on a date right now.

22  JENNIFER: Yeah. So maybe only desperate people try this

23     speed dating thing.

24  WENDY: I'm starting to feel desperate.

25  JENNIFER: Me too.

26  WENDY: But who needs a boyfriend anyway?

27  JENNIFER: Hey, at least we have each other to hang out with.

28  WENDY: That's true.

29  JENNIFER: I say we give ourselves one more round and if

30     neither of us have any luck, then we duck out of here.

31  WENDY: That sounds like a good idea to me.

32  JENNIFER: But maybe, hopefully, fingers crossed, the next one

33     will be Mr. Right for both of us.

34  WENDY: I hope so. *(Bell rings.)*

35  JENNIFER: Good luck.

1    WENDY: Good luck to you, too *(JENNIFER exits and BRADLEY*
2       *enters and sits down.)*
3    BRADLEY: My darling, it's fate!
4    WENDY: Fate?
5    BRADLEY: I look around the room and see no other.
6    WENDY: How many girls have you tried this line on?
7    BRADLEY: Darling, there is no one but you.
8    WENDY: Darling? You don't even know me.
9    BRADLEY: It's the connection. I'm feeling it.
10   WENDY: Really?
11   BRADLEY: And look at you. Look how your eyes light up as you
12      look at me. *(Touches her face.)* Your love is evident to the
13      entire world. Well, to the entire room.
14   WENDY: *(Jumps up.)* Look here, Mister ...
15   BRADLEY: Bradley.
16   WENDY: Look here, Bradley, you don't know me and I don't
17      know you. So, why don't you try talking to me in a more
18      normal way.
19   BRADLEY: Of course, of course. I'm sorry. *(WENDY sits down.)*
20      Whatever you want, my darling.
21   WENDY: *(Slams her hand down on the table.)* I'm not your
22      darling.
23   BRADLEY: *(Reaches out and touches her hand.)* Don't fret, my
24      love ... you will be.
25   WENDY: *(Yanks her hand away.)* Are you on something?
26   BRADLEY: Yes, it's called love. Love at first sight.
27   WENDY: You can't love someone you don't know.
28   BRADLEY: Not true. For so long now I have loved you from afar.
29   WENDY: For so long?
30   BRADLEY: Since we got here.
31   WENDY: *(Looks at her watch.)* You've loved me from afar for ten
32      minutes?
33   BRADLEY: Yes! Oh yes, my darling. *(Bell rings.)*
34   WENDY: Time's up.
35   BRADLEY: *(Kisses her hand.)* Until we meet again, my love. *(She*

1    *snatches her hand away. He exits.)*
2    **JENNIFER:** *(Enters.)* **That was absolutely my last date.**
3    **WENDY:** *(Stands.)* **Mine too.**
4    **JENNIFER: That last guy I talked to insisted on my phone**
5         **number and then had the nerve to tell me he would e-mail**
6         **me a calendar of the days he would be available.**
7    **WENDY: I had that one, too.**
8    **JENNIFER: Did you give him your number?**
9    **WENDY: No! Did you?**
10   **JENNIFER: Oh, I gave him a number all right.**
11   **WENDY: You did?**
12   **JENNIFER: Yes, but it wasn't mine.**
13   **WENDY: Then whose number did you give to him?**
14   **JENNIFER: The homework hotline number.** *(They share a*
15        *laugh.)* **Come on, let's get out of here.** *(They exit.)*

# 2. Play Practice

CAST: (3M, 2F) CASSIE, TRISH, SCOTT, MIKE, RAMON
PROPS: 5 scripts
SETTING: Bare stage

1     *(At rise, CASSIE, who plays Mom/Edna, and TRISH, who*
2     *plays Aunt Blythe, are on the stage reading from their*
3     *scripts.)*
4   CASSIE: The twins will be here shortly.
5   TRISH: And I can't wait to meet them.
6   CASSIE: And wait until you see how they have grown.
7   TRISH: The last time I saw them, why they were ... let me
8     see, they were ...
9   CASSIE: Three.
10  TRISH: And now?
11  CASSIE: Thirteen. Hard to believe, isn't it?
12  TRISH: My how time flies by. *(SCOTT, who plays Clyde, and*
13     *MIKE, who plays Milton, enter.)*
14  CASSIE: Look, it's the twins! Boys, come here. Aunt Blythe is
15     here to see you.
16  SCOTT: *(Looks away from script. To CASSIE)* Hey, can you say
17     I'm sixteen instead of thirteen?
18  MIKE: Which means I'm sixteen, too. Since we're twins.
19  TRISH: Guys, I don't think Mrs. Solis will let us change the
20     script.
21  SCOTT: But I don't want to be a thirteen-year-old brat.
22  MIKE: Yeah, with him as my brother.
23  SCOTT: Maybe you could say we were adopted.
24  MIKE: Different dads. But we can still be brothers.
25  CASSIE: Guys, you're twins. Same father, same age.
26  TRISH: And she should know because she's your mother.
27  MIKE: And Cassie really looks like our mom, doesn't she?
28  SCOTT: Yeah. Real believable. I still think we should be
29     sixteen instead of thirteen. So just say Aunt Blythe

1 hasn't seen us in thirteen years. We were three when
2 she last saw us, then thirteen years later ...
3 MIKE: We're sixteen.
4 CASSIE: I'm not changing the script. I don't want to get into
5 trouble.
6 TRISH: Excuse me! Can we practice our lines, please?
7 MIKE: *(Reads dryly from script.)* Aunt Blythe.
8 SCOTT: *(Reads dryly from script.)* Aunt Blythe, you're here.
9 TRISH: *(Hugs them.)* Oh, my darlings!
10 SCOTT: *(Off script)* Uh, do you have to call us your darlings?
11 MIKE: Yeah, it sounds old-fashioned. Can't you just say,
12 "Hey, what's up?"
13 CASSIE: We're supposed to be rehearsing our lines, not
14 changing them.
15 MIKE: *(Looks at script.)* Aunt Blythe!
16 SCOTT: Aunt Blythe, you're here!
17 TRISH: *(Hugs them.)* Oh, my darlings! Now, would you boys
18 like to see what I brought you from New York?
19 MIKE: New York?
20 SCOTT: New York?
21 MIKE: *(To SCOTT)* We're supposed to say that together.
22 SCOTT: OK, one, two, three ...
23 MIKE and SCOTT: New York?
24 TRISH: Yes, my darlings. Your Auntie Blythe lives in New
25 York. And look what I brought for you. A small replica
26 of the Empire State Building.
27 CASSIE: What do you say, boys?
28 MIKE: Thank you, Aunt Blythe.
29 SCOTT: Thank you, Aunt Blythe.
30 CASSIE: *(Looking at the script)* Now this is where the phone
31 rings. Ring, ring. *(Mimics answering phone.)* Hello.
32 What? No! No! Say it's not true!
33 MIKE: *(Off script)* I think this is the part where our father
34 has been killed in the war.
35 SCOTT: Oh yeah. We're supposed to look sad and start

1     **crying.** *(MIKE and SCOTT begin to cry.)*

2     **TRISH: Not yet! She hasn't told you that he's dead yet. Oh my**

3     **gosh. You guys are the worst actors.** *(Goes back to her*

4     *script.)* **Edna, what's wrong?** *(The BOYS laugh.)* **What?**

5     **MIKE:** *(Laughing)* **Edna!**

6     **SCOTT: Can you imagine naming your kid Edna?**

7     **MIKE: Or worse yet, dating an Edna?**

8     **CASSIE: Well your name is not so great, Milton!**

9     **TRISH: Yeah, who'd want to date a Milton?**

10    **CASSIE: Or a Clyde?**

11    **SCOTT: Hey, don't knock my name, Edna.**

12    **TRISH: Can we** *please* **get back to the script?** *(Looks at script.)*

13    **OK, where were we?**

14    **CASSIE: You were asking me what was wrong.**

15    **TRISH: Oh yeah.** *(Reads script.)* **Edna, what's wrong?** *(The*

16    *BOYS snicker.)*

17    **CASSIE: It's Paul.**

18    **TRISH: Is he all right?**

19    **SCOTT: He's dead!** *(Bursts out crying.)*

20    **MIKE: Our daddy is dead!** *(Cries. CASSIE and TRISH glare at*

21    *the BOYS.)*

22    **CASSIE: You don't know he's dead yet.**

23    **SCOTT: Yes I do. It says right here in the script.** *(Reads.)*

24    **Following the news, the twins, Clyde and Milton, cry as**

25    **they learn their father has died in the war.** *(To MIKE)*

26    **Let's practice, OK?**

27    **MIKE: OK.** *(They both begin sobbing as the GIRLS glare at*

28    *them.)*

29    **CASSIE: You don't know he's dead yet because I haven't said**

30    **that part yet!**

31    **MIKE: You haven't?**

32    **SCOTT: Oh, I thought you had.**

33    **TRISH: She hasn't! Oh my gosh.**

34    **MIKE:** *(Crying)* **Then tell us.**

35    **SCOTT:** *(Crying)* **Yeah! Tell us that our father is dead.**

1    CASSIE: Not until you stop crying.

2    MIKE: But we're supposed to cry. See. *(Shows the script to*

3        *her.)* The twins cry.

4    TRISH: You idiots! You don't cry until Cassie has broken the

5        news.

6    CASSIE: And I haven't broken the news yet.

7    MIKE and SCOTT: *(Stop crying.)* Oh.

8    MIKE: So? Break the news.

9    CASSIE: Why do they have to be my children?

10   TRISH: Or my nephews?

11   SCOTT: Mom ... *(Begins to cry.)* Is he dead?

12   MIKE: Yeah, Mom. *(Crying)* Is our father dead?

13   SCOTT: Tell us, Mom.

14   MIKE: Yeah, tell us, Mom.

15   CASSIE: *(To TRISH)* I'm not talking to them.

16   TRISH: Let's ignore them. They're so stupid. Definitely

17       thirteen-years-old.

18   CASSIE: For sure.

19   MIKE: Mom!

20   SCOTT: Aunt Blythe!

21   CASSIE: We'll just skip over the parts where they speak.

22   TRISH: Good idea.

23   CASSIE: *(Looking at her script)* OK, the phone is ringing.

24       Ring, ring. Hello. What? No! No! Say it's not true!

25   TRISH: Edna, what's wrong?

26   MIKE and SCOTT: *(Begin crying.)* Our father is dead!

27   CASSIE: Stop it!

28   TRISH: Cassie, just ignore them.

29   CASSIE: I'm trying.

30   MIKE: He's dead!

31   SCOTT: Our father is dead!

32   CASSIE: *(Looks at script.)* And I drop the phone then say, "It's

33       Paul."

34   SCOTT: He's dead!

35   TRISH: Scott, shut up. Ignore him, Cassie.

1 **CASSIE: It's Paul.**

2 **TRISH: Paul? What about Paul?**

3 **MIKE: He's dead!**

4 **SCOTT: He's dead?**

5 **CASSIE:** *(Glares at the BOYS, then to TRISH)* **He's dead.**

6 **TRISH: Oh, Edna!**

7 **CASSIE: What will I do? How will I ever go on?** *(MIKE and*

8 *SCOTT continue to cry and console one another as they*

9 *repeat, "He's dead. Our father is dead.")*

10 **TRISH: Oh, Edna!**

11 **CASSIE: He was shot by enemy fire.**

12 **TRISH: Oh, Edna!**

13 **CASSIE: And how will I ever tell the boys?**

14 **TRISH: Oh, Edna ...**

15 **RAMON:** *(Enters holding script. He plays Paul.)* **Hey.**

16 **MIKE: Dad!**

17 **SCOTT: Dad, you're not dead!**

18 **RAMON: Who said I was dead?**

19 **TRISH: Ramon, you're not supposed to enter during this**

20 **scene. You're dead.**

21 **RAMON: I die?**

22 **CASSIE: Ramon, haven't you even read the script?**

23 **RAMON: No. I mean, some of it.**

24 **TRISH: Well, let us break the news to you. You die.**

25 **RAMON: I die?**

26 **CASSIE: Sorry, but you die from enemy fire.**

27 **SCOTT: Our daddy's dead?**

28 **MIKE: Daddy's dead?**

29 **CASSIE: Guys, stop it.**

30 **TRISH: Really. Please.**

31 **RAMON: Really? I die?** *(MIKE and SCOTT continue to cry and*

32 *console each other.)* **Great. So if I'm dead, how am I**

33 **supposed to enter and say stuff? Am I a ghost?**

34 **MIKE:** *(Points.)* **A ghost!**

35 **SCOTT: Daddy's a ghost?**

1   **CASSIE: Stop it!**
2   **TRISH: Please!**
3   **RAMON: I'm a ghost?**
4   **TRISH: Ramon, you don't die till scene five. And that's the**
5       **scene we're rehearsing.**
6   **RAMON: Oh. Well, cool. Then I can just sit back and chill**
7       **then.** *(Sits down.)* **Don't let me stop you.**
8   **CASSIE:** *(Looks at script.)* **How will I ever go on?**
9   **TRISH: Edna, you must! For the twins. And Paul would want**
10      **you to.**
11  **RAMON: Can I say something here?**
12  **TRISH: No!**
13  **CASSIE: What?**
14  **RAMON: Well, wouldn't it be better if you just fell over and**
15      **died, too? I mean, from a broken heart.**
16  **TRISH: That's not in the script, Ramon.**
17  **RAMON: I know, but wouldn't the play be better if you died**
18      **after you found out I died?**
19  **CASSIE: No.**
20  **TRISH: And what about the twins? Then they wouldn't have**
21      **a mother or a father.**
22  **RAMON: Well, they'll have their Aunt Blythe.** *(MIKE and*
23      *SCOTT run to hug her.)*
24  **MIKE: Aunt Blythe!**
25  **SCOTT: Aunt Blythe!**
26  **TRISH: Stop it!**
27  **RAMON: And the three of you could live happily ever after.**
28  **CASSIE: But I don't want to die.**
29  **RAMON: Hey, it happens.**
30  **SCOTT: And then let's say that after our father and mother**
31      **have died, that Aunt Blythe gets run over by a train.**
32  **TRISH: Run over by a train?**
33  **MIKE: Yeah! And we're orphans.**
34  **SCOTT: Yeah!**
35  **RAMON: That's not a bad idea.**

1   MIKE: But on our way to the orphanage, we get hit by
2       a car —
3   SCOTT: And we die. We all die!
4   MIKE: Yeah!
5   RAMON: I like that.
6   CASSIE: Come on, Trish. Let's go practice somewhere else.
7   TRISH: Good idea, Cassie. Let's go. *(They exit.)*
8   MIKE: But instead of getting hit by a car, maybe we could get
9       swallowed up by lava from an explosive volcano.
10  SCOTT: Yeah! Like we're on our way to the orphanage and
11      the lava is chasing us ...
12  MIKE: And we're running and running ...
13  RAMON: But we can't run fast enough.
14  MIKE: *(Demonstrates.)* Running, but the lava is too fast!
15  SCOTT: Buried alive.
16  MIKE: Yeah! *(They fall to the ground and pretend to die.)*

# 3. How to Show Respect

CAST: (2M, 2F) MRS. WYLIE, DIEGO, AMELIA, ADAM
PROPS: Paper, pens, tissue
SETTING: Counselor's office

1   *(At rise, DIEGO is slouched in a chair as MRS. WYLIE*
2   *stands over him.)*
3 **MRS. WYLIE:** Mr. Cooper has recommended that you attend
4   my class "How to Show Respect" for the next six weeks.
5   And Diego, do you know why you've been
6   recommended for my class?
7 **DIEGO:** Yeah.
8 **MRS. WYLIE:** Yeah?
9 **DIEGO:** Because I have problems with authority.
10 **MRS. WYLIE:** *(Looks at notes.)* Talking while the teacher is
11   talking, interrupting, not being prepared for class,
12   passing notes, laughing during class ... This list goes on
13   and on, Diego.
14 **DIEGO:** Yeah.
15 **MRS. WYLIE:** That's "Yes ma'am," Diego.
16 **DIEGO:** Yeah, OK.
17 **MRS. WYLIE:** "Yes ma'am," Diego.
18 **DIEGO:** I said OK.
19 **MRS. WYLIE:** And I said you need to reply with "Yes
20   ma'am!"
21 **DIEGO:** No you didn't.
22 **MRS. WYLIE:** I'm going to have a hard time with you, aren't
23   I? *(DIEGO shrugs.)* So let me hear you say it.
24 **DIEGO:** It.
25 **MRS. WYLIE:** Excuse me?
26 **DIEGO:** You said, "Let me hear you say it." I said *it.*
27 **MRS. WYLIE:** I said let me hear you say yes ma'am.
28 **DIEGO:** No you didn't. You said, "Let me hear you say *it.*" So
29   I said *it.*

1   MRS. WYLIE: *(Through clenched teeth)* Diego, I meant let me
2       hear you say yes ma'am!
3   DIEGO: Then why didn't you say, "Let me hear you say yes
4       ma'am"? You said, "Let me hear you say it" ... so I said
5       it.
6   MRS. WYLIE: *(Screams.)* Let me hear you say yes ma'am!
7   DIEGO: But you didn't ask me a question. What would I be
8       saying yes ma'am to? If you asked me if I liked being in
9       here, I'd say no ma'am. No ma'am!
10  AMELIA: *(Enters.)* Mr. Cooper said I have to come in here.
11  MRS. WYLIE: Come in. *(To DIEGO)* I'll finish dealing with
12      you in a minute. *(To AMELIA)* Did you bring me
13      anything from Mr. Cooper?
14  AMELIA: *(Pulls out a piece of paper.)* This. But none of it's
15      true.
16  MRS. WYLIE: *(Looking at the paper)* And it appears you have
17      a problem with stealing items that are not yours.
18  AMELIA: No I don't!
19  MRS. WYLIE: So you deny stealing lunch money from your
20      fellow students?
21  AMELIA: I sure do deny it.
22  MRS. WYLIE: And you deny trying to exit the library
23      without checking out your books?
24  AMELIA: A mistake.
25  MRS. WYLIE: Stealing Mr. Griffith's stopwatch?
26  AMELIA: I borrowed it.
27  MRS. WYLIE: Natalie's coat?
28  AMELIA: Borrowed that too. I was cold.
29  MRS. WYLIE: Jimmy's cell phone?
30  AMELIA: Borrowed it. Needed to make a phone call.
31  MRS. WYLIE: Hall passes?
32  AMELIA: Borrowed.
33  MRS. WYLIE: You borrowed hall passes?
34  AMELIA: I needed the paper so I could write myself a note.
35      *Note to self: Tomorrow bring money for crazy hat day.*

1      You don't get to wear a hat if you don't bring a dollar.

2  MRS. WYLIE: Hall passes for your to-do list?

3  AMELIA: That's right.

4  MRS. WYLIE: So, not only are you a thief, but a liar as well.

5  AMELIA: I am not!

6  MRS. WYLIE: But you are going to learn some valuable
7      lessons in my six-week class. You, Amelia, will become
8      a giver and not a taker.

9  AMELIA: What six-week class?

10  DIEGO: It lasts for six weeks?

11  MRS. WYLIE: A class that I have designed myself for you
12      disrespectful thieves and liars out there. *(As if reading*
13      *a marquee)* "How to Show Respect!"

14  DIEGO: Do I have to go?

15  MRS. WYLIE: Yes sir, you do!

16  AMELIA: I have to go too?

17  MRS. WYLIE: Yes ma'am.

18  DIEGO: So what happens if I don't show up?

19  AMELIA: Yeah, what happens?

20  MRS. WYLIE: Ever heard of the word "expelled"?

21  DIEGO: Man!

22  AMELIA: You can make me go, but you can't make me listen.

23  MRS. WYLIE: Oh, you will listen, young lady. And you're
24      going to learn that teachers deserve the respect of their
25      students because they work hard to educate them. Got
26      it? And neither one of you would get anywhere in life if
27      the teachers weren't here to teach you. So, they
28      shouldn't be taken for granted or disrespected.

29  AMELIA: So how is borrowing some stupid hall passes or a
30      stopwatch disrespecting my teachers?

31  MRS. WYLIE: Did you ask to borrow those items?

32  AMELIA: Maybe.

33  MRS. WYLIE: Liar!

34  ADAM: *(Enters.)* **Mr. Cooper said I have to see you.** *(Hands*
35      *MRS. WYLIE a note.)*

1 MRS. WYLIE: *(Looks at the note.)* **And here we have Mr.**
2 **Funny Guy. Sit down, Adam.**
3 ADAM: **Hey, do you know why cannibals don't eat clowns.**
4 *(Short pause)* **They taste funny!** *(Everyone laughs except*
5 *MRS. WYLIE.)* **And how about this one? Why didn't the**
6 **skeleton cross the road?** *(Short pause)* **Because he didn't**
7 **have the guts!** *(Again, everyone laughs except for MRS.*
8 *WYLIE.)* **How about this? What was the witches' favorite**
9 **subject in school?** *(Short pause)* **Spelling!**
10 MRS. WYLIE: **E-nough!**
11 ADAM: **Want to hear another one? Knock knock.**
12 AMELIA: **Who's there?**
13 ADAM: **Ears.**
14 AMELIA: **Ears who?**
15 ADAM: **Ears looking at you.**
16 MRS. WYLIE: **Stop it!**
17 ADAM: **OK, OK.**
18 DIEGO: **Don't you want him to say yes ma'am?**
19 ADAM: **Why would I want to say yes ma'am?**
20 DIEGO: **Because she likes to hear it. Yes ma'am! No ma'am!**
21 **But don't say it. Even if she says she wants to hear it.**
22 **Which I still think is funny, but she has no sense of**
23 **humor. Which is good that you've joined our little**
24 **group here because you ought to keep us laughing.**
25 MRS. WYLIE: **Everyone shut up. *Just shut up!***
26 AMELIA: **I didn't say anything.**
27 MRS. WYLIE: **You are now.**
28 AMELIA: **So you want me to shut up?**
29 MRS. WYLIE: **Yes!**
30 DIEGO: **Yes ma'am.** *(He smiles.)* **See, I can say it.**
31 ADAM: **Why is everyone so tense?**
32 AMELIA: **Beats me.**
33 ADAM: **Want me to tell another joke?**
34 DIEGO: **Sure.**
35 AMELIA: **I love jokes. Tell us another one.**

1  ADAM: OK, there was this chicken and ...
2  AMELIA: Who crossed the road?
3  ADAM: Not that chicken.
4  DIEGO: Who laid an egg?
5  ADAM: That's the one.
6  MRS. WYLIE: No more. No more talking. No more jokes. No
7      more anything except for sitting here and zipping your
8      mouth and listening. Do you understand?
9  DIEGO: Yes ma'am.
10  MRS. WYLIE: I said to hush!
11  DIEGO: You also said to say yes ma'am.
12  MRS. WYLIE: Not now! I want you to all be quiet. Do you
13      hear me?
14  DIEGO: Yes ma'am. *(Covers mouth.)* Oops. You didn't want
15      me to say yes ma'am right then, did you?
16  AMELIA: Well, I didn't say anything.
17  ADAM: Neither did I.
18  MRS. WYLIE: On the count of three, no one says a word. One
19      ... two ... *three!*
20  AMELIA: Can I go to the bathroom?
21  ADAM: I have a good bathroom joke. Want to hear it?
22  DIEGO: Yeah! *(MRS. WYLIE storms out of the room.)*
23  AMELIA: I wonder where Mrs. Wylie went?
24  ADAM: Maybe she had to go to the bathroom.
25  DIEGO: Probably. *(We hear MRS. WYLIE scream, then after a
26      moment she enters and approaches each student
27      individually as she points at them.)*
28  MRS. WYLIE: *(To DIEGO)* Don't talk! *(To AMELIA)* Don't talk!
29      *(To ADAM)* Don't talk!
30  ADAM: But —
31  MRS. WYLIE: *(To ADAM)* No! Shhhh! *(Turns and composes
32      herself.)* Now that I have your attention and without
33      being interrupted again, I have a few things I'd like to
34      say to you. All three of you will be attending my class,
35      "How to Show Respect." Classes don't begin until next

1       Monday, but I want to give you a head start on
2       practicing what you will be learning. So let's get out
3       some paper and a pen and write down what I tell you.
4       First of all, when you are in class, you are to sit up
5       straight. So number one, sit up straight!
6 **DIEGO:** *(As he is writing)* **Sit ... up ... straight.**
7 **MRS. WYLIE: Shhhh! And let's all practice doing just that.**
8       *(Claps her hand.)* **Sit up straight.** *(THEY sit up.)* **And**
9       number two: always keep your eyes on your teacher as
10      she or he speaks. Come on. Look at me! *(THEY look at*
11      *her.)* Number three: always come to class prepared with
12      your notebook, homework, and any other required
13      items for your class. By doing this you are showing
14      respect to your teacher. Any questions? *(THEY shake*
15      *their heads.)* Teachers should not tolerate anything
16      from you other than your full attention. They have
17      spent endless hours preparing lessons for you to learn
18      and it is your responsibility as a young adult to pay
19      close attention, listen, and learn. Now, each one of you
20      needs to be in room three-oh-two at seven a.m. sharp
21      every morning for the next six weeks. And leave all
22      your personal items outside my room. No cell phones.
23      No handheld games. No gum or candy. Nothing but
24      notebook paper and pens. *(Looks at ADAM.)* And no
25      funny stuff, you hear? *(ADAM nods.)* All right then. I'll
26      see you all on Monday. Room three-oh-two. Seven a.m.
27      sharp.
28 **DIEGO: Yes ma'am!**
29 **AMELIA:** *(Hands DIEGO a pen.)* **Here's your pen. I stole it.**
30      **Sorry.**
31 **ADAM: And I have nothing funny to say. I'm a changed man.**
32 **DIEGO: That Mrs. Wylie is one tough counselor.**
33 **AMELIA: I'll never take anything that isn't mine again.**
34 **ADAM: And I'll never tell another joke in class again.**
35 **AMELIA: Honesty is the best policy.**

1  DIEGO: Yes ma'am! No ma'am!
2  AMELIA: It's the Golden Rule from now on.
3  DIEGO: Yes ma'am!
4  AMELIA: Taking what doesn't belong to you is wrong.
5  DIEGO: Yes ma'am.
6  AMELIA: What goes around comes around.
7  DIEGO: Yes ma'am.
8  AMELIA: A thief is a lowlife scum.
9  DIEGO: Yes ma'am.
10 AMELIA: I'm a new person. Thanks to Mrs. Wylie!
11 DIEGO: Yes, a new person am I. Respect is my middle name.
12     Yes ma'am. No ma'am. Yes sir. No sir. Thank you so
13     much. I'm so honored. Here, let me open that door for
14     you. Homework is completed and on time. No, I will not
15     talk to others during class. I will only pay attention. Sit
16     up straight! Look at my teacher and listen. Yes ma'am!
17 MRS. WYLIE: I have to say, I can't believe this ... this
18     transformation! *(ADAM raises his hand.)* Yes, Adam?
19 ADAM: Mrs. Wylie, I want to apologize to you for my
20     disruptive attitude earlier.
21 MRS. WYLIE: Well, thank you, Adam.
22 ADAM: I have seen the error of my ways. Jokes are not funny
23     when they are disruptive. Thank you, Mrs. Wylie. *(He*
24     *kisses her hand.)* You are the finest counselor in the
25     universe.
26 MRS. WYLIE: Oh, that's a little overboard, don't you think?
27 ADAM: No ma'am.
28 DIEGO: No, ma'am!
29 AMELIA: It's true, Mrs. Wylie. I've never learned so much
30     earth-shattering truth in my entire life. Your "How to
31     Show Respect" technique rocks. I get it. I really and
32     truly get it.
33 ADAM: As I do.
34 DIEGO: Yes ma'am! I have learned the importance of
35     respect.

1 MRS. WYLIE: I've never had such a quick come around. I'm
2     so pleased. So very pleased.
3 AMELIA: And since we've already learned our lesson ...
4 DIEGO: Yes ma'am! We have all learned our lesson.
5 ADAM: Perhaps, Mrs. Wylie, you would be so gracious to let
6     us bypass your six-week class.
7 MRS. WYLIE: What?
8 AMELIA: So you will have more time and energy to
9     concentrate on the disrespectful students who haven't
10     seen the light as we have. We, Mrs. Wylie, get it. We have
11     caught onto your dynamic teachings and we are ready
12     to go back to the classroom and practice what we have
13     learned.
14 DIEGO: I might even suggest to the journalism teacher that
15     they write an article about you in the school paper,
16     Mrs. Wylie.
17 MRS. WYLIE: Really?
18 DIEGO: Yes ma'am!
19 MRS. WYLIE: Really, I don't know what to think here.
20 ADAM: You, Mrs. Wylie, are the epitome of a great
21     counselor.
22 AMELIA: Your own program put to test ...
23 DIEGO: "How to Show Respect" ... an excellent teaching
24     program by Mrs. Wylie.
25 MRS. WYLIE: I'm just flabbergasted! And I suppose ... you
26     students really don't need to attend my six-week
27     program after all. It does appear it has sunk in. It's
28     amazing. I'm truly amazed.
29 DIEGO: You're amazing, Mrs. Wylie.
30 AMELIA: The best!
31 ADAM: I second that.
32 MRS. WYLIE: OK, OK, I'm about to tear up here. *(Dots her*
33     *eyes with a tissue.)* You kids ... Wow. If you will just
34     excuse me. And I guess I will just be seeing you around.
35     Stop by my room and say hello sometime, will you?

1   **DIEGO: Yes ma'am!**

2   **AMELIA: We will.**

3   **ADAM: Absolutely.** *(MRS. WYLIE exits.)*

4   **DIEGO: Oh, I'm so glad that we got out of Mrs. Wylie's six-**
5      **week class.**

6   **AMELIA: Me too! I don't want to get up at five-thirty a.m. to**
7      **be at her class at seven a.m. sharp.**

8   **ADAM: It would be torture. Complete torture!**

9   **DIEGO: Well, we pulled that one off.**

10  **ADAM: Sure did.**

11  **AMELIA: There was nothing to it.** *(Pause)* **Uh ... Adam, here's**
12     **your ten dollars back.**

13  **ADAM: Where did you get that?**

14  **AMELIA: I took it. Before I was a changed person.**

15  **ADAM: Thanks. I mean, thanks for being honest and giving**
16     **it back.**

17  **DIEGO: Honesty is the best policy. So, Adam, do you want to**
18     **tell us that chicken who laid an egg joke now?**

19  **ADAM: You know, I'm not really in the mood to tell a joke.**

20  **DIEGO: You know, I'm not really in the mood to hear one**
21     **either.**

22  **AMELIA: Diego, would you walk with me to the office? I**
23     **need to turn in a few hall passes that I stole.**

24  **DIEGO: Yes ma'am!**

25  **ADAM: Wait! Unless we wanted to save them for a rainy day?**

26     *(They think about this for a moment, then shake their*
27     *heads no as they start to leave.)*

28  **DIEGO: Yeah, I'm glad I don't have to attend that class. It**
29     **would have been a waste of time.**

30  **AMELIA: A complete waste of time.**

31  **ADAM: Knock knock.**

32  **DIEGO and AMELIA: Who's there?**

33  **ADAM: Orange.**

34  **DIEGO and AMELIA: Orange who?**

35  **ADAM: Orange you glad I fooled you?** *(They laugh.)*

# 4. Save Me from Myself

CAST: (2M, 1F) KYLE, JERRY, MISS GIBBS
PROPS: Masking tape, a note
SETTING: School hallway

1   KYLE: Jerry, you've got to help me. You've got to save me
2       from myself.
3   JERRY: Why? What's going on?
4   KYLE: Quick! Take this masking tape and wrap it around
5       my mouth so I can't talk.
6   JERRY: *(Takes the tape.)* OK.
7   KYLE: And listen, it's better if you don't even ask why you're
8       doing this.
9   JERRY: *(Pulling out a long strip of tape)* OK. *(Puts a piece of*
10      *tape across KYLE's mouth.)*
11  KYLE: *(Pulls the tape off.)* But aren't you going to ask me
12      why?
13  JERRY: No. You told me not to. But I do have a question.
14  KYLE: I knew it. Go ahead.
15  JERRY: OK, so when I wrap this tape across your mouth,
16      what's to keep you from ripping it off and talking
17      anyway? Like you just did.
18  KYLE: Good observation, Jerry. *(Holds out both hands.)* Here.
19      I want you to tape my hands so I can't rip the tape from
20      my mouth.
21  JERRY: OK.
22  KYLE: But aren't you going to ask me why?
23  JERRY: I know! Why don't I wrap your entire body up like a
24      mummy? That way you'd be completely prevented
25      from speaking. Otherwise, you may break free and rip
26      the tape off your mouth.
27  KYLE: Tape me up like a mummy?
28  JERRY: And I'll wrap you up really tight. *(Puts a piece of tape*
29      *across KYLE's mouth.)* But we might have one problem.

1 **KYLE:** *(Talks through the tape.)* **What?**
2 **JERRY: What did you say?**
3 **KYLE:** *(Attempts to say)* **What problem?**
4 **JERRY: Kyle, I can't understand what you're saying.**
5 **KYLE:** *(Screams through tape.)* **I said, what problem?**
6 **JERRY: Sorry Kyle, but I don't understand what you're**
7 **trying to say.**
8 **KYLE:** *(Rips the tape off his mouth, yells.)* **I said, what**
9 **problem?**
10 **JERRY: Did I say there was a problem?**
11 **KYLE: Jerry! You put the tape across my mouth then said we**
12 **might have a problem.**
13 **JERRY: Oh yeah! That.** *(Puts another piece of tape across*
14 *KYLE's mouth.)* **Well, if I'm going to wrap up your entire**
15 **body like a mummy, we may have a problem.**
16 **KYLE:** *(Through the tape)* **What problem?**
17 **JERRY:** *(Puts another piece of tape across his mouth.)* **I'm**
18 **going to need more tape. Now stand still and I'll work**
19 **with what I've got.** *(Puts another piece across KYLE's*
20 *mouth.)*
21 **KYLE:** *(Frantically pulls the tape from his mouth.)* **Jerry!**
22 **JERRY: Why did you do that? Now I'm going to have to start**
23 **all over.**
24 **KYLE: Jerry, don't you want to know** *why* **I want you to put**
25 **tape across my mouth?**
26 **JERRY: I guess. But I think it'll look cool when I'm finished**
27 **with you and you're this big massive mummy walking**
28 **around school. I wonder what the teachers will say?**
29 **The girls will probably scream.**
30 **KYLE: I wanted you to tape my mouth shut so I couldn't talk!**
31 **JERRY: Kyle, I already figured that out.**
32 **KYLE: But don't you want to know** *why?*
33 **JERRY: So you won't say something stupid, right?**
34 **KYLE: Well, I don't think it's stupid, it's just I don't know**
35 **what kind of repercussions I can expect.**

1   JERRY: Repercussions? Huh?
2   KYLE: What will happen when I blurt out my confession.
3   JERRY: Your confession? Man, don't do it! *(Rips off a piece of*
4       *tape and puts it on KYLE's  mouth.)* **Don't confess to**
5       **what you did.**
6   KYLE: *(Pulls off the tape.)* It's not what I did.
7   JERRY: What you witnessed?
8   KYLE: No, no! It's how I feel. And how can I hold it in, and
9       yet ... how can I confess it?
10  JERRY: Confess your feelings?
11  KYLE: Yes! But should I?
12  JERRY: Uh ... Why don't you let me be the judge of that?
13      Pretend I'm the person you want to confess your
14      feelings to, and I'll tell you whether it's a good idea or
15      not.
16  KYLE: OK, but this might seem a little strange.
17  JERRY: I can handle it. Go ahead.
18  KYLE: Miss Gibbs, there's something I have to tell you –
19  JERRY: Whoa! I'm your teacher? I'm Miss Gibbs? I'm a girl?
20  KYLE: This was your idea, Jerry.
21  JERRY: OK! OK! Go on.
22  KYLE: Miss Gibbs, I want to tell you how I feel.
23  JERRY: You hate her class? You can't tell her that. She'll get
24      mad.
25  KYLE: No! That's not it.
26  JERRY: You cheated? And now you feel terrible about it and
27      you want to confess to what you did?
28  KYLE: Jerry, I don't cheat. And even if I did I wouldn't
29      confess to it.
30  JERRY: Good, good. OK, I'm completely lost, but go ahead.
31  KYLE: *(Takes JERRY's hand.)* Miss Gibbs ... I love you.
32  JERRY: *(Yanks his hand away.)* Whoa! Whoa! Oh, no! No, no,
33      no! No!
34  KYLE: I shouldn't tell her?
35  JERRY: You're in love with your teacher?

1 KYLE: Yeah.
2 JERRY: Dude, that happens in elementary. You know, like
3    when you're six- or seven-years-old and you draw those
4    little heart pictures for your teacher. But the truth is
5    you just love your teacher like you love your own
6    mother. But you don't love your teacher like ... like she's
7    a girl. And she's not a girl. She's a teacher!
8 KYLE: I knew it. I shouldn't have told you.
9 JERRY: No, no! It's good that you told me. It's good. Really
10    good! Because yes, I do need to save you from yourself.
11 KYLE: I don't know how this happened.
12 JERRY: You're messed up, man.
13 KYLE: What?
14 JERRY: You're confused, that's what I meant.
15 KYLE: I don't feel confused.
16 JERRY: Look, dude, you've got to stop and think about this.
17    Miss Gibbs is like old.
18 KYLE: She's not that old.
19 JERRY: Compared to you, yes she is! She's a lot older than
20    you. And what is she going to do, date one of her
21    students? Man, she could go to jail for that.
22 KYLE: I didn't think about that.
23 JERRY: And your parents aren't going to let you date your
24    teacher.
25 KYLE: That's true.
26 JERRY: And believe me, Principal Atkins is not going to let
27    Miss Gibbs date you.
28 KYLE: I know, but —
29 JERRY: What? The two of you can have lunch together in the
30    cafeteria?
31 KYLE: I don't know. Maybe.
32 JERRY: Or swap notes between classes?
33 KYLE: *(Pulls a note from his pocket.)* I did write her a note.
34 JERRY: Give me that! *(Snatches note.)* You're not giving this
35    to her. Do you hear me?

1  KYLE: But —
2  JERRY: What were you going to do, Kyle? Stay after class and
3     proclaim your love to her?
4  KYLE: I know it was a stupid idea. That's why I grabbed this
5     tape so I would stop myself from getting humiliated.
6  JERRY: But now that you see that confessing your love to
7     Miss Gibbs is the wrong thing to do, don't you think
8     you can do without the tape?
9  KYLE: Jerry, the problem is that when I see her ... *(In a*
10     *dreamy tone)* I forget every rational thought.
11  JERRY: *(Looking over KYLE's shoulder)* Oh no. This is bad.
12  KYLE: What?
13  JERRY: Very, very bad!
14  KYLE: What? What, Jerry? *(Quickly, JERRY pulls off a piece of*
15     *tape and quickly covers KYLE's mouth. After a moment,*
16     *MISS GIBBS enters.)*
17  MISS GIBBS: Hello, boys.
18  JERRY: Hi, Miss Gibbs!
19  KYLE: *(Through the tape)* Hello, Miss Gibbs.
20  MISS GIBBS: Whatever are you boys doing?
21  JERRY: It's a ... a little experiment! Right, Kyle?
22  KYLE: *(Through the tape)* Miss Gibbs, I wanted to tell you
23     something...
24  MISS GIBBS: What did he say?
25  JERRY: Oh, he was telling you about our experiment.
26  MISS GIBBS: What kind of experiment is it?
27  KYLE: *(Through the tape)* I wanted to tell you how I feel!
28  JERRY: What kind of experiment is it?
29  KYLE: *(Puts his hand across his heart. Through the tape)* Miss
30     Gibbs, I have to confess —
31  MISS GIBBBS: What did he say?
32  JERRY: He, uh ... he wanted to tell you about our experiment.
33  MISS GIBBS: Then why doesn't he take the tape off his
34     mouth so he can?
35  KYLE: *(Pulls the tape off his mouth.)* Miss Gibbs, I wanted to

1    tell you —
2    JERRY: *(Quickly puts another piece of tape across KYLE's*
3        *mouth)* **But that would ruin our little experiment,**
4        **wouldn't it?**
5    KYLE: *(Through the tape)* **I want to tell you how I feel!**
6    MISS GIBBS: **It's a secret?**
7    JERRY: **Yes! Actually it is. A secret.**
8    MISS GIBBS: **An experiment that's a secret?**
9    JERRY: **Yes!**
10   KYLE: *(His hand across his heart, through the tape)* **Miss**
11       **Gibbs ... oh, Miss Gibbs —**
12   MISS GIBBS: **What is he trying to say?**
13   JERRY: *(Adds another piece of tape to KYLE's mouth.)* **That's**
14       **the secret.**
15   MISS GIBBS: **But I don't understand. What he's trying to say**
16       **is the secret?**
17   JERRY: **Well, we can't tell you. Because it's a secret.**
18   KYLE: *(Through the tape)* **I want to tell you —**
19   JERRY: *(Puts another piece of tape over KYLE's mouth.)* **But if**
20       **you have to know. The experiment is ... uh ...**
21   MISS GIBBS: **I'm listening.**
22   JERRY: **The experiment is to see if you can understand what**
23       **Kyle is saying while he has his mouth taped shut.**
24   MISS GIBBS: **Oh. Well, all right. Kyle, I'm listening. What**
25       **did you want to say?**
26   JERRY: *(Adds another piece of tape to KYLE's mouth.)* **Here.**
27       **Just to make sure.**
28   MISS GIBBS: **Kyle?**
29   KYLE: *(Through the tape)* **I love you!** *(Both the boys are*
30       *looking at MISS GIBBS. A pause.)*
31   MISS GIBBS: **Oh, isn't that sweet.**
32   JERRY: **You heard him? You heard what he said?**
33   MISS GIBBS: **I'm sorry, was I not supposed to? Or is it good**
34       **that I understood what he said? I'm not sure what**
35       **results you were hoping for in your little secret**

1       experiment, but I heard exactly what he said.

2   JERRY: Well, it depends. What do you think about what you

3       thought he said?

4   MISS GIBBS: Well, boys, I think that love is the greatest gift

5       of all.

6   JERRY: You do?

7   KYLE: *(Through the tape)* You do?

8   MISS GIBBS: Yes! *(Smiles.)* It's what makes the world go

9       'round. *(Exits.)*

10   KYLE: *(Frantically pulls the tape off his mouth)* Did you hear

11       that?

12   JERRY: Not at all what I expected.

13   KYLE: She loves me!

14   JERRY: Whoa! Whoa, dude! She didn't say that!

15   KYLE: She didn't say she didn't.

16   JERRY: She didn't say she did! She said love makes the world

17       go 'round.

18   KYLE: *(In a dreamy tone)* Yes, she did. Love makes the world

19       go 'round ...

20   JERRY: Yeah, love in a general way. Like, I love this school, I

21       love hot dogs, I love to skateboard, I love my teachers.

22       That kind of love.

23   KYLE: She loves me!

24   JERRY: Sure, Miss Gibbs loves you. She loves me, too. She

25       loves all of her students.

26   KYLE: I'm going to go find her and tell her again how I feel.

27   JERRY: No! No, you can't!

28   KYLE: Why not?

29   JERRY: Kyle, I'm going to do what you asked.

30   KYLE: What's that?

31   JERRY: *(Puts tape across his mouth.)* I'm going to save you

32       from yourself!

# 5. Miss Innocent

CAST: (1M, 2F) MICHELLE, DARLA, BRYAN
PROPS: 3 student desks
SETTING: A high school classroom

1   *(At rise, MICHELLE, the ghost of a high school student, is*
2   *standing at Stage Right facing the audience. An empty*
3   *school desk is behind her. At Stage Left, DARLA, a high*
4   *school student and MICHELLE's enemy, and BRYAN, a*
5   *high school student and MICHELLE's boyfriend, are*
6   *sitting very closely together in school desks.)*
7   **MICHELLE:** *(To audience)* **It really doesn't matter how it**
8   **happened, but the truth is, it happened. And how did it**
9   **happen? Well, we'll get to that in a minute. But you**
10  **know, it is kind of strange. Creepy. And spooky.** *(Makes*
11  *a "spooky" sound.)* **Kind of makes the hair on your arms**
12  **stand on end. But what else do you expect? From a**
13  **ghost! Because that's what I am. A ghost. I can see you,**
14  **but you can't see me. Which means ... I'm dead!**
15  **Expired. Kaput. Shall we say history? Oh, that's funny!**
16  **Actually, it's ironic because that's exactly where I am.**
17  **My history class.** *(Waving)* **Hey, Mr. Lewis. Mr. Lewis,**
18  **can you see me? I know I wasn't very good in your class,**
19  **but you were a great teacher.** *(Pause)* **Of course he can't**
20  **see me. What was I thinking?** *(Points to the empty chair*
21  *behind her.)* **See that empty desk over there? Well, that**
22  **was me.** *(Pause, disappointed)* **I know, I know. I can see**
23  **you, but you can't see me.** *(Suddenly points to DARLA.)*
24  **But her! Oh, I wish she could see me. Yes, you over**
25  **there, Miss Innocent. Well, it doesn't matter. Actually**
26  **it's better this way. Because I've come back here to**
27  **haunt you. That's right. It's become my one and only**
28  **true mission in life. Or shall we say death?** *(Goes to*
29  *DARLA and stands behind her.)* **Yes, that's right, Darla.**

1      I'm about to become your worst nightmare! So look
2      out. Because I'm going to follow your every move. Trip
3      you up. Mess with you head. Make you jump. And make
4      you think, "Oh my gosh! There's a ghost in the room!"
5  **DARLA:** *(Crying)* I can't believe she's gone. I know we
6      weren't friends, but I didn't want her dead.
7  **MICHELLE: Liar!**
8  **DARLA: Sure, we had our differences, but she didn't deserve**
9      **this.**
10  **MICHELLE:** *(Waves arms in front of DARLA.)* **Hello! Yes, you**
11      **right there with the innocent act. How stupid do you**
12      **think I am? And how stupid do you think Bryan is? We**
13      **can all see through your pathetic little game.**
14  **DARLA:** *(Puts her head on BRYAN's shoulder.)* **Oh, Bryan ...**
15  **MICHELLE: Hey! Stop that! Don't cry on Bryan's shoulder.**
16      **That's *my* boyfriend. *My* shoulder to cry on. Not yours.**
17  **BRYAN: I know, Darla. I miss her too.**
18  **MICHELLE: Bryan, look. Look at her! She doesn't even have**
19      **any tears. Look! So what does that tell you? It tells you**
20      **that Miss Innocent is a big fat liar. A fake, Bryan. A fake!**
21      **She's just pretending to cry so you'll put your arms**
22      **around her and comfort her.**
23  **BRYAN:** *(Puts his arms around DARLA, who is crying.)* **I know,**
24      **I know ...**
25  **MICHELLE:** ***Bryan! Don't put your arms around her and***
26      ***comfort her!***
27  **DARLA: Oh, Bryan, I wish I could take back all of those**
28      **mean things I said to Michelle.**
29  **MICHELLE: Liar.**
30  **BRYAN: Darla, I can't imagine you ever saying anything**
31      **mean to anyone.**
32  **MICHELLE: Believe it, Bryan. It's true. She said plenty of**
33      **hateful things to me during my time on earth.**
34      *(Imitates.)* **"Where did that outfit come from? A garage**
35      **sale?"**

1 DARLA: Bryan, do you think Michelle forgives me?

2 MICHELLE: No!

3 BRYAN: Of course.

4 DARLA: Because I'm really sorry for the way I treated her.

5     Do you think that she somehow senses that?

6 BRYAN: Darla, she's in a better place now. And being there,

7     she wouldn't have any anger towards you.

8 MICHELLE: Wanna bet?

9 BRYAN: She knows you're sorry for whatever it is you think

10     you did.

11 DARLA: Oh, I hope so, Bryan. I really hope so.

12 MICHELLE: *(Imitates DARLA.)* "I hope so, Bryan. I really

13     hope so." *(Pointing at DARLA)* Look here, Miss Innocent.

14     I've come back here to haunt you. Every second of

15     every day. Michelle is my name and torturing is my

16     game.

17 DARLA: And I'm sure that deep down inside, Michelle was

18     really a nice person, even though I never saw that side

19     of her. It's just ... she had this way of getting under my

20     skin, you know? She was so possessive and insecure. I

21     mean, every time I gave you a tiny little hug or said

22     hello ... she just went ballistic. And I was just trying to

23     be your friend.

24 MICHELLE: Stop your lying. You know that you wanted to

25     be more than just friends with my boyfriend. How

26     stupid do you think I am? You are such a liar. And I can

27     see right through you. *(Thinking)* Guess you can see

28     right through me, too. Well, anyway, that doesn't

29     matter now because it won't be long until Bryan sees

30     through you, too.

31 BRYAN: Darla, not everyone gets along. Some people just

32     clash. You don't have to feel bad about that.

33 DARLA: *(Holding onto BRYAN's arm)* Do you mean that?

34 BRYAN: Of course.

35 MICHELLE: Stop that. Get your slimy hands off my

1       **boyfriend! And let's just remember who cornered who**
2       **in the cafeteria and said she was going to have Bryan**
3       **for a boyfriend ... No matter what it took!** *(To the*
4       *audience)* **Did you get that? "No matter what it took!"**
5       **And what did I say? Get this!** *(Speaks slowly.)* **Pay very**
6       **close attention. I said** *over my dead body!* *(Nodding her*
7       *head)* **Uh-huh. Get it now?** *(Points to DARLA.)* **She's the**
8       **one. She did it. Miss Innocent over there did it.** *(Makes*
9       *a cutting gesture across her throat.)*
10 **DARLA: And I never thought I'd say this, but I'm actually**
11       **going to miss her. School won't be the same anymore.**
12       **Oh, Bryan ... how are we going to get through this?**
13 **BRYAN: Darla, we'll just have to find the strength.**
14 **DARLA:** *(Sniffling)* **I feel like such a baby.**
15 **BRYAN: Don't be embarrassed. It's all right.**
16 **DARLA: Guys are so strong and girls just cry like babies.**
17 **MICHELLE: Some girls cry like babies, Darla, but not you.**
18       **Because your tears are fake! Look at her, Bryan. Open**
19       **your eyes. And don't let her put her slimy hands on you.**
20       **Push her away.** *(Pauses as she watches BRYAN put his*
21       *arm around DARLA)* **Bryan! Stop it! Don't put your arm**
22       **around her. Bryan! And what was that kiss on her**
23       **forehead for? Comfort?**
24 **DARLA: Oh, Bryan, you're the only person who knows how**
25       **to make me feel better.**
26 **BRYAN: I can't stand to see you so sad, Darla.**
27 **DARLA: Oh, Bryan ...** *(Snuggles into his arms, wiping away*
28       *tears.)*
29 **MICHELLE: Bryan! Push her away. Don't you see what she's**
30       **doing? She can't replace what we had. Bryan!** *(Jumping*
31       *around, trying to get his attention)* **Hello? Remember**
32       **me? The dead girlfriend over here? Cry over me! Me!**
33       **OK? Bryan!** *(She glares at them.)*
34 **BRYAN: We should do something positive to help us deal**
35       **with our pain.**

1   DARLA: Like what?

2   BRYAN: I don't know. Plant a bush or something.

3   DARLA: That's a good idea. *(Pointing)* And we could plant it
4      right outside the window.

5   BRYAN: And when we feel sad during the school year, we
6      could look out ... and remember.

7   DARLA: Yes. That is, if we have time. Because you know how
8      Mr. Lewis is about handing out assignments.

9   BRYAN: That's true.

10  DARLA: It was nice of him to give us free time in class today.

11  BRYAN: So we could grieve.

12  DARLA: Yes. You know, Michelle never liked this class. I
13     think she was failing.

14  BRYAN: Are you serious? I didn't know that.

15  DARLA: Well, not that I like talking bad about the dead, but
16     she made terrible grades in this class. Like on Fridays
17     when we had our pop tests, she always bombed them. I
18     know because Mr. Lewis let me take up the papers.

19  BRYAN: And those were easy.

20  DARLA: I know! So, do you think it'd be right to plant a bush
21     outside the window of the class she was failing?

22  BRYAN: Well, I think it's more for us, than for her.

23  DARLA: That's true.

24  BRYAN: To honor her memory.

25  DARLA: You know, I could make a pretty ribbon to tie
26     around the bush.

27  BRYAN: That'd be nice, Darla.

28  DARLA: Hey, after school, do you want to go look for
29     something to plant? Then afterwards we could come
30     back here and have a little memorial service.

31  BRYAN: That'd be great, Darla. Thanks for being so
32     considerate and helpful.

33  DARLA: And maybe after we plant the bush and have our
34     little memorial service we could go do something fun.
35     You know, to lift our spirits.

1  BRYAN: Hey, there's a new movie out that I've wanted to see.
2  DARLA: What's that?
3  BRYAN: *Ghost Busters Three.*
4  DARLA: Oh, I heard that was good. I never saw the first two,
5      but I think that was before my time.
6  BRYAN: Hey, I know. Why don't we go and rent the first two
7      movies and watch them at my house tonight? Then
8      tomorrow we can go to the theatre and watch the third
9      one.
10 DARLA: Yeah! That's a great idea.
11 MICHELLE: *(Depressed)* Wow. I'm dead for what ... ? *(Looks at*
12     *watch.)* Twenty-four hours and you've already moved
13     on? That's fine, Bryan. Just fine. But you know what?
14     Move onto someone else. Just not Darla, OK? Not Miss
15     Innocent over there who did me in.
16 BRYAN: So it's a date?
17 DARLA: Absolutely! And don't forget, another movie date
18     tomorrow night.
19 BRYAN: *Ghost Busters Three.* Yes!
20 MICHELLE: Well, so much for claiming that you couldn't
21     live without me. Couldn't go on. Couldn't look at
22     another girl. What a joke!
23 BRYAN: *(Looks at MICHELLE's empty chair.)* But you know ...
24     *(Begins crying.)* I still can't believe that Michelle is gone.
25     I loved her so much! She was my life ... my love ... my
26     everything!
27 MICHELLE: *(Smiles.)* Now we're talking.
28 BRYAN: But I guess ... I guess ...
29 DARLA: *(Comforting him)* What? What, Bryan?
30 MICHELLE: You'll never love again, right?
31 BRYAN: I guess it just wasn't meant to be.
32 MICHELLE: *What?*
33 DARLA: Some things aren't.
34 MICHELLE: *Wasn't meant to be? Are you serious?*
35 BRYAN: And maybe, just maybe, something good will come

1        out of this horrible situation.

2   **MICHELLE:** *Situation?*

3   **BRYAN: You know I've heard that tragedies bring people**

4        **closer together. You know what I mean?**

5   **MICHELLE: Oh yes, I know exactly what you mean.** *You pig!*

6        *(Short pause as she composes herself)* **Well, I guess I'll**

7        **just have to haunt two people instead of one. Yes!**

8        **Tripping you up, ruining your plans, causing**

9        **confusion.** *(Smiles.)* **Unexplained accidents. Yes, this**

10       **might be fun. In fact, I can't wait to get started.** *(Pause*

11       *as she stares at BRYAN, who is kissing DARLA's hands.)*

12       **But could you please stop kissing her for a minute?**

13       **Please?** *(After staring at them, she buries her head in her*

14       *hands.)* **Oh, I can't stand to watch this. I wish it were**

15       **just a bad dream.** *(Lifts her head, opens eyes, yawns.)*

16       **Wow. That was a strange dream. Or was it a dream?**

17       **Maybe I wasn't dreaming. Maybe I really am ...** *(Gulp)*

18       **dead! What if I am? What if I'm standing here in front**

19       **of this entire class and they really can't see me?** *(Looks*

20       *at herself.)* **I can see me, but ... can they?** *(Quickly bolts*

21       *around in a complete circle. Then, as if speaking to Mr.*

22       *Lewis)* **No, I'm fine. I was just ... uh, daydreaming.**

23       *(Slowly she walks over to DARLA who is working on an*

24       *assignment)* **Oh, Darla?**

25   **DARLA:** *(In a hateful tone)* **What do** *you* **want?**

26   **MICHELLE: I just wanted to tell you something.**

27   **DARLA:** *(Snaps.)* **What?**

28   **MICHELLE: Well, you know how you keep throwing**

29       **yourself at** *my* **boyfriend?**

30   **DARLA:** *(Smiles.)* **Oh, is someone getting all jealous again?**

31   **MICHELLE: Well, listen here, Darla, I can see right through**

32       **you. So get this! If you ever, and I mean ever, try to steal**

33       **my boyfriend away from me, it'll be over my dead body!**

34       *(Suddenly stops, takes a deep breath as if to take it back.)*

35       **I mean ...Well, uh ... let me just say this. If you ever try**

1        **to steal Bryan away, I'll ... I'll ... I'll be really mad at you!**

2        **Got that?**

3  **DARLA: Whatever.** *(Goes back to her assignment. MICHELLE*

4        *stomps to her desk and sits down.)*

# 6. Contagious

CAST: (2M, 2F) CHLOE, DAVID, BLAKE, ASHLEY
PROPS: Several crumpled up tissues, box of tissues, books, notebooks, pens
SETTING: Library

1    *(At rise, ASHLEY sits on one side of a long table and*
2    *CHLOE, BLAKE, and DAVID sit on the other end. They are*
3    *all working on school assignments with books, notebook*
4    *paper, and pens on the table. ASHLEY sneezes, gets a*
5    *tissue, and repeats this several times. Several crumpled*
6    *up tissues are on the table in front of her.)*
7   **CHLOE:** *(To the BOYS)* **She should've stayed home.**
8   **DAVID: Yep. I sure don't want her germs.**
9   **CHLOE: Me neither.**
10 **BLAKE: I do.**
11 **DAVID: What?**
12 **BLAKE: I mean ... if Ashley and I were a couple ... I wouldn't**
13    **mind.**
14 **CHLOE: You and Ashley?**
15 **BLAKE: I said** *if* **—**
16 **DAVID:** *(Pats BLAKE on the back.)* **Well, you just dream on,**
17    **buddy!**
18 **BLAKE: Thanks.** *(ASHLEY sneezes.)*
19 **CHLOE: Why didn't she stay home?**
20 **DAVID: Major essay due on Friday. "Stress and its effect on**
21    **young people today." No less than five thousand words.**
22 **BLAKE: Mrs. Ripley is causing me a great amount of stress**
23    **by making me write this essay. Yeah, I think I'd like to**
24    **get sick. Then I could have an extension on this stupid**
25    **paper.** *(Suddenly)* **Hey! That's a great idea.**
26 **CHLOE: What's a great idea?**
27 **BLAKE: If I could get Ashley to breathe on me, or better yet,**
28    **sneeze on me —**
29 **DAVID: Blake, you're an idiot.**

39

1   CHLOE: I agree.

2   BLAKE: No, no, it's perfect! I get sick, stay home for a few

3       days, stay in bed, sleep, watch TV ... *and* get a nice long

4       extension on my essay. And I need it because I haven't

5       even started. What's the topic again? Stress and how it

6       stresses us?

7   DAVID: "Stress and its effect on young people today."

8   BLAKE: Yeah, that.

9   CHLOE: You haven't even started?

10  BLAKE: No.

11  CHLOE: Then what have you been working on?

12  BLAKE: A drawing of Godzilla. *(Holds up his artwork, then in*

13      *a deep voice)* Who could win against Godzilla? Nobody!

14      Godzilla, the body of a tyrannosaurus, the long arms of

15      an iguanodon. And the dorsal fins of a stegosaurus.

16      Teeth like steel hooks. The strength of an army. And

17      Godzilla's powerful weapon ... his atomic breath! Only

18      a few blasts of this fire was all it took to destroy

19      Mechagodzilla and Spacegodzilla.

20  DAVID: Cool.

21  CHLOE: You've been drawing this entire time? Five

22      thousand words due on Friday and you're drawing a

23      picture of Godzilla? Oh my gosh!

24  BLAKE: Relax. I've practically written the essay in my head.

25      Stress and ... and ... what? How it makes you ... forgetful?

26  DAVID: "Stress and its effect on young people today."

27  BLAKE: Yeah, that. *(Stands.)* I'll be back.

28  CHLOE: Wait. If you're going over there where Ashley is,

29      don't come back over here and contaminate the rest of

30      us.

31  BLAKE: What? You don't want my germs? Or make that

32      *Ashley's* germs?

33  DAVID: I don't want your germs, but I want her germs.

34      *(Looking adoringly at ASHLEY)*

35  BLAKE: You don't want an extension on the essay? Essays

1     and how they stress you out?
2  DAVID: I'm halfway finished.
3  BLAKE: No staying in bed, sleeping, and watching TV for a
4     couple of days?
5  DAVID: My mom would hover over me the whole time. No
6     thanks.
7  BLAKE: Well, have it your way. Wish me luck.
8  CHLOE: Good luck that you get sick?
9  BLAKE: Yes siree!
10  CHLOE: Blake, you're so stupid.
11  DAVID: I agree with Chloe. *(BLAKE sits next to ASHLEY.)*
12  ASHLEY: *(Sneezes.)* I wouldn't sit here if I were you.
13  BLAKE: You want to see the picture I drew of Godzilla?
14  ASHLEY: Did you not ... *(Sneezes)* ... hear what I said? I'm
15     probably contagious.
16  BLAKE: Great!
17  ASHLEY: Great?
18  BLAKE: I mean ... it's a great day, isn't it?
19  ASHLEY: Not when you feel like this. *(Takes a deep breath as*
20     *if she's about to sneeze, but tries to hold it.)*
21  BLAKE: Go ahead. Let it out. Just let it out!
22  ASHLEY: What?
23  BLAKE: Let out a big sneeze. Let your germs fly everywhere!
24     *(Pause)* Go ahead. Sneeze. *(Pause)* Aren't you going to?
25  ASHLEY: It passed. I don't need to now. Shouldn't you be
26     sitting over there with your friends?
27  BLAKE: No. I'm fine.
28  ASHLEY: You won't be if you get this illness from me. *(About*
29     *to sneeze)*
30  BLAKE: *(Moves in closer.)* Go ahead. *(Puts his arm around*
31     *her.)* Just let it out.
32  ASHLEY: What are you doing?
33  BLAKE: Helping you.
34  ASHLEY: Sneeze?
35  BLAKE: Supporting you.

1   **ASHLEY:** Why?

2   **BLAKE:** I'm just that kind of guy. So go ahead. Sneeze!

3   **ASHLEY:** *(Shakes her head.)* No. I'm over it.

4   **BLAKE:** *(Moves in closer.)* So tell me, Ashley ... have you ever
5       kissed a guy in the library?

6   **ASHLEY:** No! Why would you ask me that?

7   **BLAKE:** What if I told you that my friends over there have
8       dared me to kiss you?

9   **ASHLEY:** Here?

10   **BLAKE:** Yes.

11   **ASHLEY:** Now?

12   **BLAKE:** Yes.

13   **ASHLEY:** *(Blows her nose.)* But I'm sick.

14   **BLAKE:** It's all right. I don't care.

15   **ASHLEY:** Why would your friends dare you to kiss me?

16   **BLAKE:** Why?

17   **ASHLEY:** Yes, why?

18   **BLAKE:** To, uh ... uh ... join their club.

19   **ASHLEY:** What club?

20   **BLAKE:** The uh ...uh ...

21   **ASHLEY:** What club?

22   **BLAKE:** *(Quickly)* The Kissing Club!

23   **ASHLEY:** The Kissing Club? I've never heard of that.

24   **BLAKE:** Yes, well, uh ... you see ... it's a club where you are
25       dared to kiss people. And if I want to be a member ...

26   **ASHLEY:** You have to kiss me?

27   **BLAKE:** Exactly!

28   **ASHLEY:** *(Goes back to working on her assignment.)*
29       Interesting.

30   **BLAKE:** *(After a pause)* Well?

31   **ASHLEY:** Well maybe you should join the Athletics Club or
32       the Homemaking Club. Because you're not kissing me.
33       Sorry.

34   **BLAKE:** OK. OK. Then you kiss me. *(Points to his lips.)* Just
35       one little peck right here. Or it can be long. One kiss

1    and I'm in. *(Puckers up.)*
2    ASHLEY: *(Back to her assignment)* No thank you.
3    BLAKE: Please! Just one little kiss?
4    ASHLEY: No.
5    BLAKE: Please!
6    ASHLEY: No!
7    BLAKE: OK, fine. Hey, can I borrow your pen?
8    ASHLEY: Why?
9    BLAKE: Just for a minute.
10   ASHLEY: Why?
11   BLAKE: I just want to touch it.
12   ASHLEY: Because?
13   BLAKE: To, uh ... see how it feels.
14   ASHLEY: Wait a minute. Are you trying to get sick?
15   BLAKE: Yes. Yes, I am.
16   ASHLEY: And that's why you wanted me to sneeze on you?
17   BLAKE: Yes. So the truth is out, so go ahead. Just give me
18      one big sneeze right in my face.
19   ASHLEY: And it's also the reason you wanted to kiss me? Not
20      to join the so-called Kissing Club?
21   BLAKE: It's true. I lied. I'm sorry.
22   ASHLEY: And it's why you wanted to touch my pen?
23   BLAKE: Yes! I want your germs. I want to get sick. I want to
24      get an extension on my essay. I want to stay home and
25      watch TV.
26   ASHLEY: *(Shakes head.)* Well, good luck. *(Stands.)*
27   BLAKE: Wait! Where are you going?
28   ASHLEY: I'm taking my germs elsewhere.
29   BLAKE: But wait! I still need you to sneeze on me. *(She exits.*
30      *He moves over and sits in her chair and takes several*
31      *deep, slow breaths.)* Come to me, you germs. Come to
32      me. *(He notices her crumpled up tissues and picks them*
33      *up and rubs them all over his face.)* Ahhhh ... yes! Germs.
34      *(A pause. He sneezes, then smiles. Stands. Sneezes again.*
35      *Then in a sickly manner)* I'm sick! I need to go home.

# 7. Excuses

CAST: (1M, 2F) EMMA, JULIA, RYAN
PROPS: Spiral notebook, phone
SETTING: Outside school

1    *(At rise, EMMA reads off a spiral notebook that JULIA is*
2    *holding up for her to see as she speaks on the phone.)*
3 **EMMA:** *(Reading dryly)* **Hi Jason, this is Emma. I would like**
4    **to thank you for asking me to the dance. As I told you**
5    **yesterday, I would get back to you and that's why I'm**
6    **leaving you this message. Unfortunately, I'm unable to**
7    **go to the dance with you. Uh ... hold on a minute.**
8    *(Covers phone with hand.)* **Where's my excuse?**
9 **JULIA:** *(Quickly turns a page in spiral notebook. Points.)* **Here.**
10 **EMMA: Thanks.** *(Into the phone)* **Sorry, I'm back. Anyway,**
11    **what I was saying is that unfortunately I'm unable to go**
12    **to the dance with you ...** *(Leans forward as she reads off*
13    *the spiral)* **And without going into a long explanation,**
14    **let me just explain by telling you that my mother has**
15    **passed away. Hold on please.** *(Quickly covers phone with*
16    *hand.)* **My mother passed away?**
17 **JULIA: I decided that sounded more believable than your**
18    **shopping spree in Paris.**
19 **EMMA: Julia, couldn't you have at least warned me first so I**
20    **could have sounded upset about it?**
21 **JULIA: Oh, sorry. Just add a little crying and sniffling to your**
22    **message.**
23 **EMMA:** *(Shakes head, into the phone, sniffling.)* **Jason, I'm**
24    **back. Sorry about that. I was just ... overwhelmed with**
25    **grief.** *(Cries.)* **Oh, she's gone, Jason. She's gone! It's so**
26    **hard. You know? Losing a mother. And anyway ...**
27 **JULIA:** *(Pointing to the notebook)* **Here.**
28 **EMMA:** *(Reading off the spiral notebook)* **Anyway, since I'll be**
29    **shopping in Paris for the week ...** *(Covers phone with*

1     *hand)* **Shopping in Paris for the week?!**

2   **JULIA: Oops! I meant to scribble that out. Skip this part.**

3   **EMMA:** *(Into the phone)* **I'm sorry, I'm so upset I don't know**

4     **what I'm saying.** *(JULIA gives her a thumbs-up.)* **So as**

5     **you can see, my schedule is just too busy to attend the**

6     **dance with you now that I have to plan a funeral. Uh ...**

7     **hold on.** *(Covers phone with hand.)* **And how will I**

8     **explain myself when I show up at the dance with Ryan?**

9   **JULIA:** *(Points.)* **Here.**

10  **EMMA:** *(Into the phone. Reads.)* **Anyway, since I'll be**

11     **shopping in Paris for the week ...** *(Covers phone.)*

12     **Shopping in Paris for the week?!**

13  **JULIA: Sorry! I meant to scribble that out, too.** *(Points.)* **Skip**

14     **to this part.**

15  **EMMA:** *(Into the phone)* **I'm sorry, Jason. I'm just so upset I**

16     **don't know what I'm saying.**

17  **JULIA: That's good!**

18  **EMMA: Shhhh!** *(Into phone)* **Anyway, my schedule is far too**

19     **busy to attend the dance with you. With the funeral**

20     **plans and all ... you know? Uh ... hold on, please.** *(Covers*

21     *phone.)* **Again, how do I explain it when I show up to**

22     **the dance with Ryan?**

23  **JULIA: We'll worry about that later. You can say something**

24     **like it was a last minute decision to go to the dance**

25     **after all. Like you went to your mother's funeral, and**

26     **then decided you needed a little pick-me-up. A little**

27     **fresh air. A break from the house. Something like that.**

28  **EMMA: And if I wear a black dress ...**

29  **JULIA: Jason will think you came straight from the funeral**

30     **to the dance.**

31  **EMMA: Yeah! OK. A little black dress is what I'll wear.** *(Into*

32     *the phone)* **I'm back. Sorry.** *(Fakes crying.)* **I'm so sorry.**

33     **It's just hard. You know? My mother dying and all. Now**

34     **where was I?**

35  **JULIA:** *(Points to notebook.)* **Here.**

1     EMMA: So anyway, since I'll be in Paris ... *(Gives JULIA a look)*
2        I mean, at my mother's funeral! *(Covers phone.)* You
3        should have changed all the shopping in Paris to
4        attending my mom's funeral before I called him, Julia!
5     JULIA: I'm sorry! I forgot! Besides, it was a last minute
6        decision.
7     EMMA: One you made without me.
8     JULIA: I'm sorry, but I thought it sounded more believable
9        this way.
10    EMMA: Well, you should have asked me about it since you
11        were killing off my mother.
12    JULIA: I didn't kill your mother.
13    EMMA: Well, it seems that way to me.
14    JULIA: Then change the story to your bratty brother.
15    EMMA: Oh, and just say I meant it was my brother who died
16        and not my mother?
17    JULIA: Say you were upset and you got confused.
18    EMMA: You're right. I am upset! *(Into the phone)* Sorry,
19        Jason. I was having a moment. You see, I'm not
20        thinking clearly. In fact, earlier I believe I misquoted. It
21        wasn't my mother who died, but my brother. Yes, it was
22        my brother who died.
23    JULIA: Cry. Come on. Cry! Cry into the phone.
24    EMMA: I'm not crying over my brother. *(Suddenly realizes*
25        *she didn't cover the phone and quickly covers it.)* I'm not
26        crying over my brother! *(Into the phone)* Jason, I mean,
27        I'm not crying over my brother in front of you. I don't
28        want you to hear me cry.
29    JULIA: That's good!
30    EMMA: Shhhh! So anyway, where was I?
31    JULIA: Here. *(Points to notebook.)* Say this.
32    EMMA: And since I'll be in Paris ... I mean ... at my mother's
33        funeral ... no, I mean ... at my brother's funeral ... I don't
34        believe I'll be able to go to the dance with you. I hope
35        you understand. I mean, after all, how many

1       opportunities does a girl have to go to Paris? I mean, to

2       a funeral. I mean ... I'll talk to you later, Jason. Bye!

3       *(Hangs up.)* That was a complete disaster.

4  JULIA: At least you got out of going to the dance with Jason.

5       And you were nice about it.

6  EMMA: Nice? I lied, Julia.

7  JULIA: Emma, just call it a little exaggeration.

8  EMMA: A little exaggeration? I lied and now I feel terrible!

9  RYAN: *(Enters.)* Hey.

10 EMMA: Ryan!

11 JULIA: Hey, Ryan.

12 RYAN: Uh, listen, Emma, I'm sorry to tell you this, but I have

13       to back out of our date to the dance on Friday.

14 EMMA: What? Why?

15 RYAN: Well, the truth is ... you're not going to believe this —

16 JULIA: Was there a death in the family?

17 RYAN: No. Why would you ask such a question?

18 JULIA: Forgot you had an African safari lined up?

19 RYAN: No.

20 JULIA: Then what's the excuse?

21 RYAN: Emma, when I asked you to the dance, I forgot I'd

22       already asked someone else. How stupid is that?

23 EMMA: What?

24 JULIA: Are you serious?

25 RYAN: *(Shrugs.)* Call me stupid.

26 JULIA: *Stupid!*

27 RYAN: I'm really sorry about this, Emma. Obviously I can't

28       take two girls. I mean, I could, but I don't think that'd

29       work out.

30 JULIA: So you're saying that when you asked Emma to the

31       dance you forgot you'd already asked someone else?

32       Really?

33 RYAN: Yeah. Something like that.

34 JULIA: Yeah, I bet it was something like that.

35 RYAN: Emma, can you forgive me?

1   EMMA: Sure.

2   RYAN: Thanks. See ya. *(He exits.)*

3   EMMA: Now what am I going to do? I just broke off my date

4       with Jason so I could go with Ryan, and Ryan just broke

5       off his date with me so he could go with someone else.

6       Now I don't get to go at all! And I'm not going alone.

7   JULIA: Emma, you could go alone.

8   EMMA: No!

9   JULIA: Or ...

10  EMMA: Or?

11  JULIA: Or you could call Jason back.

12  EMMA: Call him back?

13  JULIA: Do it! I'll help you explain.

14  EMMA: OK. *(Dials.)* I'll have to leave him another message

15      since he's still at football practice.

16  JULIA: Perfect.

17  EMMA: *(Into phone)* Hey. Jason, it's me, Emma. I'm sorry to

18      call you again, but, uh ... hold on. *(Covers phone.)* What

19      am I supposed to say?

20  JULIA: That you made a mistake.

21  EMMA: *(Into the phone)* Jason, I made a mistake.

22  JULIA: It was a joke.

23  EMMA: *(Into the phone)* It was a joke.

24  JULIA: Laugh.

25  EMMA: *(Into phone)* Laugh.

26  JULIA: No! Laugh!

27  EMMA: *(Into phone)* Oh! *(Laughs.)*

28  JULIA: Now just go with it. Improvise. I got you through the

29      first part of it.

30  EMMA: *(Laughing)* It was a joke. Uh ... See, my brother didn't

31      die. Sometimes I wish he would, but that's another

32      story. *(Laughs.)* So the truth is, I can go with you to the

33      dance. Since I'm not going to Paris and my mother

34      didn't die and my brother didn't die and ... Well, just

35      thank God! So anyway, pick up me at seven. OK? OK.

1      **Bye!** *(Hangs up.)* **That was awkward.**
2   JULIA: At least you have a date now.
3   EMMA: I may still wear that little black dress to the dance.
4   JULIA: That'd look nice. And now you don't have to fake
5         looking sad from just leaving your mother's ... or make
6         that brother's funeral.
7   EMMA: True. And next time, maybe we can come up with a
8         better excuse.
9   JULIA: Shopping in Paris was a little overboard.
10  EMMA: True.
11  JULIA: How about next time you can't go because you have
12        to wash your hair.
13  EMMA: Like that's believable.
14  JULIA: Or you could try Ryan's excuse.
15  EMMA: Yeah! I'm sorry, Jason, but when I said I'd go with
16        you I forgot I'd already agreed to go with someone else.
17  JULIA: Yeah, but who'd ever believe that one?
18  EMMA: I wouldn't.
19  JULIA: Me neither. That Ryan is such a liar.
20  EMMA: So was I. So next time, I'll just stick with the truth.
21  JULIA: Jason, I can't go to the dance with you because I had
22        a better offer.
23  EMMA: No, that sounds mean. So, maybe I'll go back to the
24        shopping in Paris.
25  JULIA: Good idea.

# 8. When Coyotes Howl

CAST: (1M, 1F) GRACE, PHILLIP
SETTING: Drama classroom

1    *(At rise, GRACE and PHILLIP are standing in front of the*
2    *classroom about to perform a duet.)*
3    **GRACE:** *(To the audience)* **Phillip and I wrote our own duet**
4        **to perform. He plays the part of Hank and I play the**
5        **part of Grace. And yes, I know my name is Grace, but I**
6        **thought that would be all right. So it's Hank and Grace.**
7        **Phillip and me ... Grace.**
8    **PHILLIP: Tell them the title.**
9    **GRACE: Oh! It's called "When Coyotes Howl" by Grace**
10       **Patterson and Phillip Jones. We hope you enjoy it.**
11   **PHILLIP:** *(Looks down and clears his throat.)* **Grace, I don't**
12       **know what we're gonna do about those dang coyotes**
13       **gettin' into the chicken house.**
14   **GRACE: Hank, don't you let me hear you swear!**
15   **PHILLIP: I didn't swear. Did I?**
16   **GRACE: You said d-a-n-g!**
17   **PHILLIP: Did I? Oh. Well, I'm sorry. Well anyway, Grace, we**
18       **lost another three chickens last night.**
19   **GRACE: I know, Hank. Which means we have t' do**
20       **somethin'!**
21   **PHILLIP: I know. Because at this rate, we won't have any**
22       **chickens left.**
23   **GRACE: And no chickens means no eggs.**
24   **PHILLIP: Yep, I've gotta do somethin'. Grace, I was thinkin'**
25       **... I could sit outside with my shotgun and −**
26   **GRACE: Hank, no! You're not gonna kill them.**
27   **PHILLIP: But they're killin' our chickens, Grace.**
28   **GRACE: Then build a better chicken house, Hank.**
29   **PHILLIP: Well, I figure them coyotes will still figure a way**
30       **in. I thought I did a pretty good job before with that**

1    chicken coop, but them coyotes always figure a way in.
2  GRACE: Well, Hank, I figure you better do somethin' else
3       then.
4  PHILLIP: I'm tryin' t' figure that out, Grace. Before them
5       coyotes eat all our chickens! 'Cause no chickens
6       means —
7  GRACE: No eggs! I tell ya what, Hank, I'm sick t' death of
8       hearin' them coyotes howl at night. It just sends chills
9       up my spine.
10 PHILLIP: Yep, they're howlin' after an evening of preyin' on
11      all those animals. Rabbits, chicken, foxes, I suspect
12      sometimes cats —
13 GRACE: Cats?
14 PHILLIP: Well, sure, Grace. Them coyotes don't care if they
15      eat your pet. They'll eat a cat just as easy as they'll eat
16      one o' them chickens.
17 GRACE: Stupid coyotes.
18 PHILLIP: Yep, they wait until it's good and dark and then
19      they venture out to attack their prey.
20 GRACE: Poor little unsuspecting animals.
21 PHILLIP: There might be a little white rabbit with a pink
22      twitchy nose just sittin' there munchin' on a blade o'
23      grass when all of a sudden *(Demonstrates)* **gotcha!**
24 GRACE: Oh, Hank!
25 PHILLIP: The coyote snatches that rabbit and takes off with
26      it. Its little legs floppin' out of his mouth, tryin' t' break
27      free as the coyote runs off into the dark night.
28 GRACE: Hank, I did not want t' hear that.
29 PHILLIP: And then the coyote stops. And then —
30 GRACE: Did you hear what I said, Hank? I do not want t'
31      hear this.
32 PHILLIP: And then he tears into that rabbit. Like this.
33      *(Demonstrates.)* **Suppertime!**
34 GRACE: Hank! Are you tryin' t' make me cry?
35 PHILLIP: Rabbit! Yum!

1   GRACE: *(Out of character)* **Phillip, what are you doing?**

2   PHILLIP: *(Still in character)* **Eatin' a rabbit.**

3   GRACE: **This is not part of the script.**

4   PHILLIP: *(Proudly, as if holding something up)* **Look! A rabbit**

5     **foot. Think I should keep it for good luck?**

6   GRACE: **What are you doing?** *(PHILLIP howls like a coyote.)*

7     **Phillip, what are you doing?**

8   PHILLIP: **Howling at the moon.** *(Howls.)*

9   GRACE: **This is not in our script!**

10  PHILLIP: *(Leans over. Out of character)* **Go with it!** *(Howls*

11    *again.)*

12  GRACE: *(Under her breath)* **No. You get back to the original**

13    **script. This is for a major grade, you idiot.**

14  PHILLIP: **I'm just getting into the character, OK?**

15  GRACE: **Just stick to the script, Phillip!** *(Looks at the*

16    *audience and smiles.)* **Hank, what are we gonna do**

17    **about those dang coyotes?**

18  PHILLIP: **Grace! Did you just cuss?**

19  GRACE: **Did I? Oh my! I believe I did.**

20  PHILLIP: *(Out of character)* **That definitely wasn't in the**

21    **script.**

22  GRACE: **I'm trying to get us back on track, Phillip!**

23  PHILLIP: **Leave that up to me.**

24  GRACE: **Phillip, if we get a bad grade on this duet, I'm**

25    **blaming you.**

26  PHILLIP: **Yep, Grace, we gotta do somethin' 'bout them**

27    **dang coyotes.**

28  GRACE: **Stop cussin', Hank.**

29  PHILLIP: **Sorry, Grace.**

30  GRACE: **So, what are you planning t' do, Hank?**

31  PHILLIP: **What am I plannin' t' do? Well, I plan t' take care**

32    **of those dang coyotes, that's what I plan t' do.**

33  GRACE: **Phillip ... I mean, Hank ... stop cussing. I mean it!**

34    *(PHILLIP howls.)* **I cannot believe you're killing our**

35    **script like this.**

1   PHILLIP: Adding a little to the script. That's all. *(Howls.)*

2   GRACE: *(Trying to get back to the script)* **So Hank** ... what do

3       ya think about settin' out a trap for them coyotes?

4   PHILLIP: A trap?

5   GRACE: Yes, a trap.

6   PHILLIP: Well, I reckon I could give that a try. But ya know,

7       Grace, we might trap somethin' else instead.

8   GRACE: Like what?

9   PHILLIP: Like our dog Jack.

10   GRACE: Then we can't do that.

11   PHILLIP: Well then, I reckon we better figure somethin' out

12       then. 'Cause I don't think I want ol' Jack gettin' caught

13       up in a trap. Yep, I figure the only thing left t' do is pull

14       out my shotgun.

15   GRACE: Kill them?

16   PHILLIP: Grace, it's either them coyotes or our chickens.

17   GRACE: But, Hank —

18   PHILLIP: Darlin', don't you worry. You just stay in the house

19       and work on your quilt. I'll be standin' outside

20       protectin' what's ours.

21   GRACE: But I hate t' see an animal die.

22   PHILLIP: You won't see a thing, Grace. You may hear the

23       shotgun blast, but if you do, you just cover your ears.

24   GRACE: And you'll get rid of it before I go outside the next

25       mornin' t' fetch them eggs?

26   PHILLIP: Course I will, darlin'. Don't you worry 'bout that.

27   GRACE: Hank, did ya hear that?

28   PHILLIP: The coyotes. They're howlin' again.

29   GRACE: Oh, I hate that sound.

30   PHILLIP: Don't you worry, Grace. I'm goin' t' protect our

31       chickens ... and you. *(He puts his arm around GRACE.)*

32   GRACE: Oh, Hank! *(She puts her head on his shoulder.*

33       *PHILLIP begins howling again. Now she is out of*

34       *character.)* **Phillip, what are you doing?! That was the**

35       **end of our scene. Stop it!** *(PHILLIP continues.)* **Stop!**

1    *(Steps away from him and looks at the audience. Smiles.)*
2    **I hope you've enjoyed our duet, "When Coyotes Howl."**
3    *Phillip!*

# 9. Babysitting Teenagers

CAST: (2M, 5F) SUE, BAILEY, LAUREN, DYLAN, AYDEN,
HANNAH, MADISON
PROPS: Purse, cell phone, sheet of paper, DVD, sack, bowl
SETTING: Living room

BAILEY: Mrs. Carter, I hope you don't mind, but I brought
my friend Lauren to help me baby-sit.

1 SUE: That's fine, Bailey. In fact, it's probably good because
2 Hannah has a little friend over to play. Which means
3 you two will have your hands full with four little
4 angels.

5 LAUREN: How old are your children, Mrs. Carter?

6 SUE: Well, Hannah is twelve. No wait, she's thirteen. Dylan
7 is fourteen and Ayden is fifteen. They insist they don't
8 need a babysitter anymore, but I don't like leaving the
9 children at home unattended. You know?

10 BAILEY: But ... my mother said you had little children. I
11 thought they'd be two- or three-years-old.

12 LAUREN: Your children are thirteen, fourteen, and fifteen?

13 SUE: Call me overprotective, but I don't like leaving my
14 babies at home without adult supervision. Oh, I need
15 to grab my purse. I left it in the kitchen. I'll be right
16 back. *(Exits.)*

17 LAUREN: Does Mrs. Carter know that we're sixteen-years-
18 old?

19 BAILEY: My mother told her.

20 LAUREN: And she wants two sixteen-year-olds babysitting
21 her kids? Her kids who are only one to three years
22 younger than us?

23 BAILEY: This is crazy! And I swear, my mom told me that
24 Mrs. Carter had three young children.

25 LAUREN: Maybe because Mrs. Carter talks about her
26 children as if they are five-years-old. And if your

1       mother never met them, she probably just assumed
2       they were young.
3  BAILEY: I guess. But this is going to be so awkward.
4       Babysitting teenagers?
5  LAUREN: Well, hopefully they'll all stay in their rooms and
6       do their own thing while we hang out and watch TV.
7  BAILEY: I hope so.
8  SUE: *(Enters with her purse.)* All right, girls, I'll probably be
9       gone shopping for several hours. And I've left all my
10      contact numbers and emergency numbers on the
11      refrigerator. And don't hesitate to call me if you need
12      anything. All right?
13  BAILEY: Yes ma'am.
14  LAUREN: Yes ma'am.
15  SUE: It's nice to go shopping without three children
16      hanging on your leg, you know?
17  BAILEY: Your kids hang on your leg?
18  SUE: Oh, it's just an expression. But it's the constant, "Mom,
19      mom, mom! Will you buy us this? Will you buy us that?
20      I'm hungry! I need to go to the bathroom!"
21  LAUREN: You still have to take your kids to the bathroom?
22  SUE: My point is I can't get any shopping done when the
23      children go with me. They want money, they want food,
24      and they want to venture off and go another direction.
25      And I don't feel comfortable letting them roam the
26      mall with all the crazies out there. You know? So when
27      my kids want to go to the mall, we go as a team. They
28      might not like it, but I care about their safety. Anyway,
29      today I'm going to do some shopping without the
30      babies hovering around me.
31  BAILEY: The babies?
32  LAUREN: The babies who are thirteen, fourteen, and
33      fifteen?
34  SUE: Precious little angels they are, but they can be a
35      handful. Especially out shopping. And since it's getting

1      close to Christmas, I can't exactly shop with them
2      hovering around, can I?
3  BAILEY: No ma'am.
4  LAUREN: I guess you can't.
5  SUE: *(Hands BAILEY a sheet of paper.)* Bailey, here's a list of
6      all the dos and don'ts for the children. And all the
7      contact numbers and emergency numbers, which are
8      also posted on the refrigerator, but you can't be too
9      careful, can you? And as you will see here, the children
10     are absolutely prohibited from sodas, sugar, and TV.
11     Call me strict, but I don't care to have mindless apes
12     running around the house. And again, under no
13     circumstances do you allow any sodas, sugar, or TV.
14     Understand?
15 BAILEY: No TV?
16 SUE: That's right. I believe in limiting their TV time. It just
17     warps the brain. Not to mention the filth that comes
18     across those electromagnetic waves.
19 LAUREN: The what waves?
20 SUE: Because studies have shown that watching TV gives
21     you brain fog.
22 BAILEY: Brain fog?
23 SUE: A relaxed meditative state that is associated with
24     suggestibility. And that's where those commercials
25     come in. Telling my babies they need to buy this or
26     that. *(Clutches her purse.)* I only buy what's good for my
27     darling babies.
28 LAUREN: Uh ... that's good.
29 SUE: And too much TV induces low alpha waves in the
30     human brain.
31 LAUREN: It does?
32 SUE: Yes! And too much time in the low alpha wave state can
33     cause the inability to concentrate. And do you think
34     that would be good for my children's schoolwork? No!
35     Yes, I do my research.

1   BAILEY: *(Under her breath)* **I'm glad my mother doesn't do**
2       **her research.**
3   LAUREN: *(Under her breath)* **Me too!**
4   SUE: **It's like staring at a blank wall for hours. Mindless.**
5       **Such a waste of time. So as I wrote down right here, no**
6       **TV. And I mean it. No TV at all!**
7   BAILEY: **Yes ma'am.**
8   SUE: **All right then. Well, I'm leaving. Call me. Call me if you**
9       **need anything at all.** *(Exits.)*
10  LAUREN: **Those poor kids.**
11  BAILEY: **I'd die if I couldn't have at least four to six hours of**
12       **TV every day.**
13  LAUREN: **Oh, me too.** *(DYLAN and AYDEN run into the room,*
14       *past BAILEY and LAUREN.)*
15  DYLAN: **Is she gone?**
16  AYDEN: **Yes, I believe she is gone. But first, a little test just to**
17       **make sure.** *(Hollering)* **Mom! Mom!**
18  DYLAN: *(Hollering)* **Mom! Oh, Mom!**
19  AYDEN: **She's gone.**
20  DYLAN: **Hello, TV.**
21  AYDEN: *(Holding up a DVD)* **The movie of all movies. A**
22       **psychopathic teacher terrorizes a high school in one of**
23       **the most horrifying slasher films ever.**
24  DYLAN: **A gore movie with heavy emphasis on the gore.**
25  AYDEN: **With shocking and violent scenes.**
26  DYLAN: **The horror movie of all movies.**
27  AYDEN: **Let the fun times begin! I'll just pop this DVD into**
28       **the player ...**
29  BAILEY: **Uh, excuse me.**
30  AYDEN: **Oh, are you the babysitter?**
31  LAUREN: **Yes, we are.** *(The BOYS laugh.)*
32  DYLAN: **I'll get the popcorn.**
33  BAILEY: *(Snatches the DVD from AYDEN's hand.)* **No TV.**
34       **Sorry.** *(Hands the DVD to LAUREN.)*
35  LAUREN: *(Looking at the DVD)* **Oh, I wanted to see this.**

1   AYDEN: *(Takes the DVD from LAUREN.)* **Here's the deal. You**
2   **stay out of our way and we'll stay out of your way.**
3   **Watch the movie with us if you want. But we don't need**
4   **a babysitter.**
5   DYLAN: **Yeah. I'm fourteen and Ayden is fifteen. And you**
6   **are ...?**
7   BAILEY: **Uh ... twenty.**
8   AYDEN: **Really?**
9   BAILEY: **Uh-huh.**
10  LAUREN: *(Likes this idea.)* **Yeah, I'm twenty, too. But I'll be**
11  **twenty-one on my birthday next week.**
12  AYDEN: **Yeah right. Haven't I seen you both at Lincoln High?**
13  BAILEY: **Must've been my sister.**
14  LAUREN: **Well, you probably saw me. I'm a student teacher.**
15  AYDEN: **Right. Sure.** *(To DYLAN)* **Go get the popcorn and**
16  **sodas, Dylan.**
17  BAILEY: **Wait.** *(Grabs the DVD.)* **No TV.** *(Looks at sheet of*
18  *paper.)* **No sodas. But the popcorn is OK.**
19  DYLAN: **Who wants popcorn without a soda?**
20  BAILEY: **I'm sorry. I'm just doing my job.**
21  DYLAN: **Man, this sucks.**
22  AYDEN: **Hold on there, buddy. I'll get this worked out.**
23  DYLAN: **But we've been waiting all week for Mom to go**
24  **shopping and leave us alone to have some fun. And you**
25  **even borrowed the DVD from Jessie just for this special**
26  **occasion.** *(To BAILEY and LAUREN)* **Look, my brother is**
27  **taller than you and if you don't cooperate with us he**
28  **can —**
29  AYDEN: *(Interrupting)* **Calm down, Dylan. Let me handle**
30  **this.** *(HANNAH and MADISON enter the room.)*
31  HANNAH: **Is she gone?**
32  MADISON: **I don't see her. I bet she is.**
33  HANNAH: *(Hollering)* **Mom! Mom! Mom! Oh, Mom!**
34  DYLAN: **Hannah, she's gone.**
35  HANNAH: **Perfect! Because Madison came over to watch**

1    some TV with me.

2  MADISON: *(Holding up a sack)* And I brought tons of candy
3      for us to snack on. Jelly beans, Sour Patch Kids, malt
4      balls, jaw breakers ...

5  HANNAH: Let's see what's on TV.

6  AYDEN: Hold on, Hannah. Dylan and I have plans to watch
7      a DVD. *(Snatches movie from BAILEY.)*

8  DYLEN: Yeah, with blood and guts. Lots of screaming!
9      Teenage kids running through the school halls
10     searching for a way out, but there is no way out.

11  HANNAH: That sounds terrible.

12  AYDEN: You and Madison wouldn't like it.

13  HANNAH: Ayden, Madison came over here just to watch TV
14      with me.

15  MADISON: And I brought candy.

16  AYDEN: And I borrowed this DVD from Jessie to watch today
17      while Mom was out shopping.

18  DYLAN: And guess what, girls? We were here first.

19  HANNAH: No! We're watching TV. And we're not watching
20      that scary movie you borrowed.

21  DYLAN: First come, first serve.

22  AYDEN: Plus, I'm older, so I get to call it first.

23  MADISON: Hannah, is there not another TV in your house?

24  HANNAH: No, just this one because Mom likes to limit our
25      TV time.

26  DYLAN: Alpha waves numb the brain.

27  AYDEN: Brain fog.

28  HANNAH: Waste of time.

29  DYLAN: As if staring at a blank wall for hours.

30  AYDEN: And I say ... bring it on! Turn on the tube.

31  DYLAN: Yeah, 'cause we've only got a few hours to get this
32      done. Good-bye, Mother. Hello, television.

33  HANNAH: Excuse me, but ladies first. TV time here we
34      come.

35  MADISON: With lots of candy.

36  AYDEN: Sorry girls, but it's not your lucky day. The boys

1      have beat you here. So run along and play with your
2      dolls or whatever it is you girls do.
3  HANNAH: No, Ayden. Madison came over here to watch TV.
4  AYDEN: And I borrowed this DVD for us to watch.
5  DYLAN: And I'm watching it with him.
6  HANNAH: That's not fair.
7  AYDEN: Life's not fair, little sister.
8  HANNAH: I'm telling Mom.
9  DYLAN: Tell Mom that we're fighting over who gets to watch
10     the TV?
11  AYDEN: Won't fall for that one, Hannah.
12  BAILEY: Uh ... excuse me.
13  HANNAH: Then I'll tell her you were watching TV while she
14     was out shopping. And I'll tell her it was rated R. That'll
15     get you grounded for sure.
16  BAILEY: Uh ... if I might interrupt ...
17  LAUREN: Excuse us, but we're your babysitters and we have
18     something to say. *(To BAILEY)* What are we going to say?
19  AYDEN: You're a brat, Hannah, you know that?
20  HANNAH: Whatever!
21  AYDEN: *(Mimics.)* Whatever!
22  BAILEY: How about a compromise?
23  DYLAN: How can we compromise? There's only one TV?
24  MADISON: Good point, Dylan.
25  HANNAH: And I'm not compromising with him.
26  AYDEN: Goes both ways here.
27  BAILEY: As your babysitter, let me suggest we do something
28     else.
29  AYDEN: No. I want to watch this movie. Besides, no sixteen-
30     year-old babysitter is going to tell me what to do. And
31     you know, the more I think about it, we have chemistry
32     together at Lincoln don't we?
33  BAILEY: Well, I, uh ...
34  AYDEN: We do. That's where I know you. Mr. Franklin's
35     chemistry class. So, how did you do on that pop quiz on

1    Friday?

2    BAILEY: I, uh ...

3    AYDEN: I was the only one at my table who nailed it. Do you

4        know Matt Sanders who sits next to me? Zero!

5    LAUREN: I'm in that same class. Only a different period.

6        That pop quiz was hard. I only made a forty.

7    DYLAN: I thought you said you were a student teacher.

8    LAUREN: Oh, well, I ... uh ... test myself ... and I ... uh ...

9        thought it was a bit hard for the students. *(Laughs.)*

10       Couldn't even pass it myself.

11   HANNAH: Can we watch TV now? I've missed TV. I'm dying

12       for TV! I think I'm going to collapse if I don't have some

13       TV time soon.

14   BAILEY: I understand, but as your babysitter —

15   HANNAH: Madison and I don't need a babysitter!

16   DYLAN: Neither do I!

17   AYDEN: Which is why we all need to agree that our mother

18       is a fanatic worrier and she just doesn't get it.

19   HANNAH: I agree with that.

20   DYLAN: Me too. I mean, me three.

21   AYDEN: So let's do as Bailey suggested and compromise.

22   LAUREN: Great idea.

23   BAILEY: Thank you.

24   HANNAH: So Ayden, what do you suggest?

25   AYDEN: Popcorn, sodas, candy. Are we all in agreement?

26   HANNAH: Yes.

27   MADISON: I am.

28   DYLAN: I'm in.

29   BAILEY: *(Holding up the list)* No! Wait! It says right here —

30   AYDEN: *(Takes the sheet of paper and crumples it up.)* Forget

31       that.

32   LAUREN: But it was your mother's instructions.

33   HANNAH: Whatever.

34   DYLAN: Yeah, whatever.

35   AYDEN: So here's what we do. We watch the scary movie

1    first, then we'll watch whatever you girls want to

2    watch. Chick flicks or whatever. Deal?

3  MADISON: Hannah, I think it'd be fair.

4  HANNAH: Well, OK. As long as Madison and I get to watch

5    whatever we want afterwards.

6  AYDEN: Deal.

7  LAUREN: Oh, and I've been wanting to see that movie.

8  AYDEN: Then maybe you better sit by me. You might want

9    me to hold your hand during the really scary parts.

10  LAUREN: OK.

11  BAILEY: But —

12  HANNAH: And let's turn out all the lights.

13  MADISON: And close the curtains.

14  DYLAN: I'll go get the popcorn. *(Exits.)*

15  BAILEY: But —

16  LAUREN: Don't worry about it, Bailey. We tried and we

17    failed. We can't control a bunch of teenagers.

18  BAILEY: Well, I guess you're right. And I do want to see that

19    movie, too.

20  LAUREN: I've heard it's really scary.

21  BAILEY: Me too.

22  MADISON: Who wants some Sour Patch Kids?

23  AYDEN: You got any chocolate?

24  MADISON: Malt balls. You like those?

25  AYDEN: Love 'em!

26  MADISON: Here you go. *(Hands him a few pieces of candy.)*

27  AYDEN: Thanks.

28  DYLAN: *(Enters with a bowl of popcorn.)* **Popcorn, candy,**

29    **scary movie ... here we come!** *(AYDEN mimes putting*

30    *the DVD into the player and ALL sit down and stare*

31    *straight ahead. Short pause)*

32  AYDEN: This is going to be good. And watch out, girls, it

33    starts out scary! At least that's what Jessie said.

34  DYLEN: Look at that.

35  AYDEN: Look at that long axe she's holding in her hands. I

1      **think she's going into the classroom. Ah, man ... what is**
2      **she going to do?**

3  **HANNAH: I'd hate to have her for a teacher.**

4  **MADISON: Me too.**

5  **DYLAN: Oh my gosh! Look!**

6  **BAILEY: Oh! I can't look!** *(The GIRLS hover down and*
7      *partially close their eyes.)*

8  **DYLAN: I'm almost afraid to look.**

9  **MADISON: The students don't even see her yet.**

10 **LAUREN: Because she's coming up from behind them.**

11 **HANNAH: Oh no!**

12 **BAILEY: Why won't they turn around and look?**

13 **HANNAH: Turn around! Turn around!**

14 **MADISON: Yeah! Turn around! Your teacher's about to**
15     **bring the axe down on you!**

16 **BAILEY:** *(Covering her eyes)* **Oh, I can't look!**

17 **LAUREN:** *(Covering her eyes)* **Me neither!**

18 **SUE:** *(Suddenly rushes into the room, from behind them)* **I**
19     **forgot my cell phone!** *(ALL jump and scream, including*
20     *SUE.)*

# 10. Seriously Overdue

CAST: (3F) SHELBY, JENNA, MISS PRUITT
PROPS: Library book, three one-dollar bills
SETTING: Outside the school library

1  (*At rise, JENNA stands nervously outside a door, holding*
2  *a library book. SHELBY enters.*)
3  **SHELBY:** Hey, Jenna.
4  **JENNA:** Hey, Shelby.
5  **SHELBY:** Are you going in the library?
6  **JENNA:** (*Takes a deep breath.*) I can't decide.
7  **SHELBY:** Is there some reason you wouldn't want to go into
8    the library?
9  **JENNA:** Yes.
10 **SHELBY:** What is it? What's wrong? Oh, wait. I know. I bet
11   there's someone in there that you don't want to see or
12   you don't want them to see you. How about this? You
13   can walk behind me and then you can duck into one of
14   the rows of books. And if you need something, just
15   whistle and I'll get you what you need. Like this.
16   (*Attempts to whistle.*) Well, I can't whistle, but hopefully
17   you can. When my ex-boyfriend Keefer and I broke up,
18   I did everything in my power to avoid him like the
19   plague. Come on. I'll hide you.
20 **JENNA:** No! I don't think I can go in there.
21 **SHELBY:** Why not? Who are you afraid of seeing?
22 **JENNA:** Miss Pruitt.
23 **SHELBY:** The librarian?
24 **JENNA:** Uh-huh.
25 **SHELBY:** And you don't want to see Miss Pruitt because ... ?
26 **JENNA:** (*Holds up book.*) I'm late returning this book.
27 **SHELBY:** So what? Just pay the fine. And Miss Pruitt is
28   always thrilled to collect those library fines, so she'll be
29   very happy to see you. So come on.

1    JENNA: No! No, I can't.

2    SHELBY: What's the matter? You need a loan? I've got a few
3        dollars I can let you borrow.

4    JENNA: Thanks, Shelby. But a few dollars wouldn't cover my
5        fine.

6    SHELBY: Uh-oh. Kept it out over a week, huh?

7    JENNA: Something like that.

8    SHELBY: At seventy-five cents a day, it can add up. I once
9        had to pay six dollars. My mom about had a conniption
10        for me not being responsible. Made me clean the entire
11        house to pay off my library fine.

12    JENNA: Yeah, well my book is seriously overdue.

13    SHELBY: How seriously overdue? More than a couple of
14        weeks?

15    JENNA: Yes.

16    SHELBY: Ouch. A month? Let's see, a month of late charges
17        would be about twenty-two dollars. Wow. That would
18        be bad. Do you have twenty-two dollars?

19    JENNA: It's going to be much more than that.

20    SHELBY: Jenna, just how late is your book?

21    JENNA: Three hundred and fifty-two days.

22    SHELBY: *(Loudly)* Three hundred and fifty-two days?!

23    JENNA: Shhhh! I don't want Miss Pruitt to hear.

24    SHELBY: *(Quietly)* Three hundred and fifty-two days? That's
25        almost a year!

26    JENNA: I know.

27    SHELBY: Three hundred and fifty-two days times seventy-
28        five cents .... *(Trying to figure it out in her head)*

29    JENNA: It's two hundred and sixty-four dollars.

30    SHELBY: *(Loudly)* Two hundred and sixty-four dollars?!

31    JENNA: Shhhh!

32    SHELBY: *(Quietly)* That's more than the cost of the book!

33    JENNA: I know.

34    SHELBY: So you haven't been to the library in a year?

35    JENNA: I snuck in a couple of times, but that's it. Other than

1         that I go to the public library or use my home computer
2         for research.
3  SHELBY: Wow! No wonder you're nervous about going into
4         the library. *(Loudly)* Two hundred and sixty-four
5         dollars!
6  JENNA: Shhhh!
7  SHELBY: What are you going to do?
8  JENNA: I don't know. I don't have two hundred and sixty-
9         four dollars. What do you think Miss Pruitt is going to
10       do to me?
11  SHELBY: I don't know. Maybe she'll set up a payment plan
12       for you. Hopefully interest free.
13  JENNA: That means I'd be paying on a school library loan
14       even after I graduate from high school. It'll be like a
15       student loan that never seems to get paid off.
16  SHELBY: Maybe you could ask your parents for the money.
17       You know, with lot of tears.
18  JENNA: Crying would be the easy part. But I can't ask my
19       parents for the money. I'd be in serious trouble.
20  SHELBY: Well, maybe deep down inside Miss Pruitt has a
21       heart.
22  JENNA: You think so?
23  SHELBY: Maybe. Just say, *(Crying)* Miss Pruitt, I'm so sorry. I
24       couldn't find the book. It was my mother's fault.
25  JENNA: My mother's fault?
26  SHELBY: She picked it up by accident and then put it in the
27       family bookshelf. I didn't know that and I couldn't find
28       it anywhere! Then the other day when I was looking for
29       a book, lo and behold, there it was. I found it! Oh, Miss
30       Pruitt, I'm so sorry. I take all the blame and I so
31       appreciate you understanding.
32  JENNA: *(Holds out her hand as if she's MISS PRUITT.)* That'll
33       be two hundred and sixty-four dollars.
34  SHELBY: But Miss Pruitt, I'm a student. I don't have that
35       kind of money.

1  JENNA: No excuses. I want my money.

2  SHELBY: But I don't have that kind of money. *(Takes out*

3      *three dollars.)* But I do have three dollars. Here! Take

4      this and we'll call it even.

5  JENNA: *(Takes the money.)* And now you owe me two

6      hundred and sixty-one dollars.

7  SHELBY: Then consider it a payment. I'll bring you a few

8      dollars every week until this fine is paid in full.

9  JENNA: I don't accept payments.

10  SHELBY: But —

11  JENNA: Does this look like a bank or a library to you?

12  SHELBY: But Miss Pruitt, surely you understand that two

13      hundred and sixty-four dollars is a lot of money for a

14      high school student.

15  JENNA: Not my problem. *(Holds out her hand.)* Pay up,

16      please.

17  SHELBY: An I.O.U.?

18  JENNA: No! And checks are not accepted either. But I do take

19      Visa, MasterCard, and American Express.

20  SHELBY: But I don't have a credit card.

21  JENNA: Not my problem.

22  SHELBY: Surely there's something I can do to take care of

23      this fine.

24  JENNA: *(Holds out her hand.)* Cash works.

25  SHELBY: I could work here. In the mornings and after

26      school. Yes! Put me to work. I'll shelve your books and

27      do whatever else you want me to do.

28  JENNA: I don't need a helper. Besides, I have students who

29      do all that work for class credit. The only thing that you

30      can do to solve this problem is hand me two hundred

31      and sixty-four dollars. In cold cash.

32  SHELBY: But I'm telling you, I don't have that kind of

33      money.

34  JENNA: Then maybe you should go to the bank and get a

35      loan.

1    SHELBY: Get a loan for a library fine?
2    JENNA: Get a loan, rob a bank ... I don't care how you do it.
3        But I want my money!
4    SHELBY: OK, OK, there has to be a solution here. One I
5        haven't thought of.
6    JENNA: Jail.
7    SHELBY: Jail? They can put you in jail for a library fine?
8    JENNA: Absolutely!
9    SHELBY: Really? Jail? But I'm returning the book! And look,
10        it's in good shape, too. No torn pages. No dog-eared
11        pages. And I didn't write in it, either. It's like brand
12        new. See?
13    JENNA: Pay up or it's jail time for you, missy.
14    SHELBY: OK, OK, I'll pay up. I just need a little time. To uh
15        ... get that loan.
16    JENNA: I'll give you till the end of the day.
17    SHELBY: The end of the day? That's it?
18    JENNA: Yes. That's it. Till the end of the day. Or ... well, you
19        know!
20    SHELBY: *(Breathing heavily)* Jail? Come on, Jenna. Let's get
21        out of here. I don't want you to go to jail over a stupid
22        book.
23    JENNA: I don't either.
24    SHELBY: Come on!
25    MISS PRUITT: *(Suddenly appears in the doorway.)* **What is all**
26        **this noise I'm hearing outside my library?**
27    SHELBY: Oh! We ... uh ...
28    JENNA: *(Attempts to hide the book.)* **We're sorry, Miss Pruitt!**
29    MISS PRUITT: **And what is this?** *(Grabs the book and looks at*
30        *it. Opens the book.)* **Jenna Davis?**
31    JENNA: Yes ma'am?
32    MISS PRUITT: **Do you realize that this book is three**
33        **hundred and fifty-two days late?**
34    JENNA: No. I mean, yes. I mean ... I'm sorry, Mrs. Pruitt!
35    MISS PRUITT: **Do you realize how much the fine is for a**

1     book this late?
2  SHELBY: Miss Pruitt, we'll get you the money by the end of
3      the day. Come on, Jenna.
4  MISS PRUITT: Hold on a minute! This book is a classic. Did
5      you know that?
6  JENNA: Yes ma'am.
7  MISS PRUITT: Which was donated to us by the Women's
8      League for Literature. You can't just check out books
9      and not bring them back.
10 JENNA: I know, Miss Pruitt. And I'm sorry!
11 MISS PRUITT: So you're going to have to pay a fine, Jenna
12     Davis.
13 JENNA: Yes ma'am.
14 SHELBY: And we'll get it to you by the end of the day. Come
15     on, let's go.
16 MISS PRUITT: Hold on! Hold on! Jenna, you have until the
17     end of this semester to pay your fine.
18 JENNA: The end of the semester? Really.
19 MISS PRUISS: That's right. End of the semester.
20 JENNA: Thank you, Miss Pruitt.
21 MISS PRUITT: And I'm afraid to tell you this, but you're
22     going to owe me twelve dollars.
23 JENNA: Twelve dollars? That's it?
24 SHELBY: Not two hundred and sixty-four dollars?
25 MISS PRUITT: Two hundred and sixty-four dollars? Where
26     did you get an amount like that?
27 SHELBY: Well at seventy-five cents a day times three
28     hundred and fifty-two days —
29 MISS PRUITT: We can't charge more than the book is worth.
30     How silly is that?
31 SHELBY: Really?
32 MISS PRUITT: Twelve dollars by the end of the semester.
33     And Miss Davis, next time ... return your book on time.
34 JENNA: Yes ma'am.
35 MISS PRUITT: And keep it down out here. This is a library,

1      **you know!** *(She exits.)*
2    **JENNA: I'm not going to jail! I'm not going to jail!** *(GIRLS*
3      *jump up and down screaming.)*
4    **MISS PRUITT:** *(From Off-Stage)* **Quiet, please!**

# 11. Use Only as Directed

CAST: (1M, 2F) NATHAN, EMILY, RILEY
PROPS: Handheld mirror, white makeup for face, two
   hairbrushes, acne cream, washrag
SETTING: Bathroom

1    *(At rise, NATHAN's face is hidden as he looks into a*
2    *handheld mirror. He has white dots all over his face. His*
3    *sister, EMILY, enters the bathroom.)*
4   **NATHAN:** *(Putting the mirror down)* **Hey! Excuse me. The**
5    **bathroom door was shut. Have you ever heard of**
6    **knocking?**
7   **EMILY: Oh my gosh! What happened to you?**
8   **NATHAN: Get out.**
9   **EMILY: Is that chickenpox?**
10  **NATHAN: Get out!**
11  **EMILY: No, it couldn't be chickenpox, because you already**
12    **had chickenpox. In fact, you gave it to me when I was**
13    **five.** *(Steps back.)* **So what's wrong with you?** *(Covers her*
14    *mouth.)* **Are you contagious?**
15  **RILEY:** *(Enters.)* **What's going on?**
16  **NATHAN: Can a guy ever get a little privacy around here?**
17    **Emily, will you and your friend please excuse**
18    **yourselves?**
19  **RILEY: Oh my gosh!** *(To EMILY)* **Is your brother sick? What's**
20    **wrong with him?** *(Covers her mouth.)* **Are you**
21    **contagious?**
22  **EMILY:** *(Still covering mouth)* **I don't know, but I hope not.**
23  **RILEY: I'd die if I woke up looking like that.**
24  **EMILY: Me too.**
25  **NATHAN: I'm not contagious.**
26  **EMILY: How do you know?**
27  **RILEY:** *(Still covering mouth)* **Yeah, how do you know?**
28  **NATHAN: All I wanted was twenty minutes in the bathroom.**
29    **Alone!**

1   EMILY: I'm sorry, but I needed my hairbrush.

2   NATHAN: *(Hands her a hairbrush.)* **Here.**

3   EMILY: Not that one. The other one.

4   NATHAN: *(Hands her another hairbrush.)* **Here. Now, would**

5        **you both get out of here? Please!**

6   RILEY: Are you sure you're not contagious?

7   EMILY: Oh no! *(Drops brush.)* I just touched his germs.

8   RILEY: And the homecoming dance is next week. What if ...

9        oh my gosh ...

10   EMILY: Oh my gosh! What if I look like that?

11   NATHAN: For the last time, I'm not contagious.

12   RILEY: *(Still covering mouth)* How do you know?

13   EMILY: *(Still covering mouth)* Yeah, how do you know?

14   NATHAN: I know because I'm the one who put this stuff on

15        my face. *(Picks up a tube of acne cream.)* Acne cream.

16        Duh!

17   EMILY: *(Uncovers her mouth.)* You did that to yourself?

18   RILEY: *(Uncovers her mouth.)* Why?

19   NATHAN: Why? *(Holds up tube.)* Acne cream for acne. Duh!

20   RILEY: But Nathan, you're only supposed to leave that acne

21        cream on for a minute or two or redness and swelling

22        will occur. Did you not read the directions?

23   NATHAN: What?

24   RILEY: Let me see that. My brother uses this same stuff.

25        *(Takes acne cream and reads.)* If the product is left on

26        your skin for more than one minute, severe burning

27        and redness will occur.

28   NATHAN: What?

29   RILEY: *(Reads.)* Rub product onto infected area, and then

30        quickly remove. The quick absorbing product will be

31        released into the skin. Within twenty-four hours, you

32        should see dramatic results.

33   EMILY: Nathan is going to have dramatic results all right.

34        Redness, swelling ...

35   RILEY: *(Reads.)* Warning: If product is left on infected area

1       for more than one minute, damage to the skin might be
2       permanent.
3  **NATHAN:** What? *(Finds a washrag and begins rubbing face.)*
4  **RILEY:** *(Reads.)* And if this does occur, you need to seek
5       medical help immediately.
6  **EMILY:** Oh, this is bad. Should I call nine-one-one?
7  **NATHAN:** *(Still wiping face)* Permanent damage? What have
8       I done?
9  **RILEY:** *(Reading)* The redness and burning might not be
10       visible immediately, but if you notice any pain
11       whatsoever, please seek immediate help as the flesh
12       will soon begin to erode and this could spread to other
13       areas of your body.
14  **NATHAN:** *(Frantically washing face)* My skin is going to
15       erode?
16  **EMILY:** That'd be gross if your skin started melting off like
17       in that movie, *Aliens Under Fire.*
18  **NATHAN:** *(Furiously rubbing face with rag)* What have I
19       done?
20  **EMILY:** Is your skin burning?
21  **RILEY:** It looks red.
22  **EMILY:** But is it burning?
23  **NATHAN:** I don't know. I don't think so. But maybe. Maybe
24       it is.
25  **EMILY:** Do you want me to call nine-one-one?
26  **NATHAN:** No!
27  **RILEY:** Well ... at least you won't have any more pimples.
28  **NATHAN:** But what if I don't have a face?
29  **RILEY:** Good point.
30  **EMILY:** Nathan ...
31  **NATHAN:** *What?*
32  **EMILY:** I'll still love you.
33  **NATHAN:** *(Looks in the hand mirror.)* What if any minute
34       now my face starts to melt away from this harsh
35       chemical?

1   RILEY: How long did you leave it on your face?

2   NATHAN: *(Looks at watch.)* Fifteen ... maybe twenty minutes.

3      *(GIRLS shake their heads.)* But I didn't know you

4      couldn't leave it on. Whoever heard of that? I thought

5      you put it on and left it on ... maybe even overnight!

6      *(GIRLS shake their heads.)* I mean, who reads the fine

7      print? And who's ever heard of putting an acne cream

8      on your face then wiping it off in at least sixty seconds

9      or ... or ... your face melts off!

10  EMILY: Like in *Aliens Under Fire.*

11  NATHAN: I'm going to look like an alien! *(Suddenly)* Tell me.

12  RILEY: What?

13  EMILY: What?

14  NATHAN: Is my face melting off? Tell me! Tell me the truth.

15      Oh God, just tell me the truth.

16  EMILY: No.

17  RILEY: At least not yet.

18  NATHAN: *(Grabs mirror.)* No, I can't look. What was I

19      thinking not to read the instructions?

20  RILEY: *(Offers him the acne cream.)* Do you want to read it

21      now?

22  NATHAN: No! And I thought, hey, the more the better. Right?

23      Glob it on, dry up the pimples, and tomorrow I'd look

24      ... *(Cries into the washrag.)* Tomorrow I won't have a

25      face!

26  EMILY: Nathan ...

27  NATHAN: *(Crying)* **What?**

28  EMILY: Mom will still love you, too. We both will.

29  NATHAN: I'll never go to school again.

30  RILEY: At least you won't be spending so much time in the

31      bathroom anymore. You won't want to look at your ...

32      well your lack of ... well ... you know what I mean.

33  NATHAN: The boy with no face!

34  RILEY: Maybe you can see a plastic surgeon.

35  EMILY: Mom wouldn't let him do that.

1   **NATHAN: Why not?**

2   **EMILY: It'd be too expensive. Man, I'm never using that stuff**

3       **when I get pimples. Let me see that.** *(Takes tube from*

4       *RILEY.)* **And I'm going to be sure to warn all my friends.**

5       **Let's see ... what's this called.** *(Reads.)* **Acne B-Gone. Safe**

6       **for all skin types. All natural ingredients with added**

7       **moisturizers.**

8   **NATHAN: Why would they put a moisturizer into a product**

9       **that's going to burn your face off?**

10   **RILEY: Yeah, that's strange.**

11   **NATHAN: Unless ...** *(Grabs tube.)* **You were lying!**

12   **EMILY:** *(To RILEY)* **You lied?**

13   **RILEY:** *(Smiling)* **Exaggerated.**

14   **NATHAN:** *(Reads.)* **Safe for all skin types. All natural**

15       **ingredients with added moisturizers. Apply liberally as**

16       **needed. For increased effect, apply at bedtime and**

17       **leave on overnight.**

18   **RILEY: That was funny, wasn't it? Gotcha!**

19   **NATHAN: Why you ... !** *(Chases RILEY Off-Stage.)*

20   **EMILY:** *(Picks up hand mirror and looks at herself.)* **I hope I**

21       **never get pimples. Wait. What's that? Oh my gosh! It's a**

22       **zit. Oh my gosh! I have a zit. My very first zit.** *(Puts*

23       *down mirror and hollers.)* **Mom! Mom!** *(Looks back in*

24       *the mirror.)* **I'm breaking out.** *(Finds cream and puts it*

25       *on her face.)* **I have a zit.** *(Lowers mirror to show white*

26       *cream on her face.)*

# 12. Zebra Hamsters

CAST: (2M) JOHN, DRAKE
SETTING: School hallway

1 JOHN: Drake, you wouldn't believe the dream I had last
2     night.
3 DRAKE: Wait, let me guess. Gina finally saw the light and
4     you two hooked up.
5 JOHN: I wish.
6 DRAKE: Or I know. Your dad walked in your bedroom and
7     handed you the keys to a new Corvette ZR1! The stuff of
8     legends. Code-named Blue Devil! Six hundred and
9     thirty-eight horsepower, V-nine engine that can
10     accelerate from zero to sixty in three point four
11     seconds.
12 JOHN: No.
13 DRAKE: And he said, "Son, it's yours. All yours. So here, take
14     the keys. No more riding the bus for you. From here on
15     out, my son will drive to school in style."
16 JOHN: I wish. That would be a dream come true.
17 DRAKE: Or I know. It's Jefferson fourteen, Fort Davis
18     fourteen, and the quarterback throws the ball, it
19     spirals in the air, the crowd is on their feet, and you're
20     running, running ... and you catch it! And there you go,
21     turning, twisting, fighting off this tackle, that tackle,
22     breaking another tackle ... And is he in? Is he in? *He's*
23     *in! Touchdown!* Jefferson wins! Rah! Rah! Rah!
24 JOHN: You know, you've got a very good imagination. But
25     that wasn't my dream.
26 DRAKE: So what did you dream about? Wait, I know! You
27     aced Mrs. Graham's English class.
28 JOHN: You're getting closer, but you need to go the other
29     direction.
30 DRAKE: Oh, a nightmare. You failed, didn't you? Summer

1      school. Uh-oh. Your self-conscious is warning you. You
2      know, preparing you for what's to come. And summer
3      school ... man, it's the pits.
4  JOHN: Drake, do you want to hear what I dreamed about?
5  DRAKE: Yeah! Tell me.
6  JOHN: OK, so picture this. Hundreds of hamsters are
7      running all over my room.
8  DRAKE: Cool!
9  JOHN: But not just any ordinary hamster, but hamsters with
10     zebra stripes.
11  DRAKE: Zebra stripes?
12  JOHN: Yeah! Hamsters that look like miniature zebras.
13  DRAKE: Awesome!
14  JOHN: So anyway, these little zebra hamsters are running
15     all over my room. And I mean everywhere. On the
16     floor, the bed, my dresser, my desk ... And I'm sitting at
17     my desk trying to write an essay for Mrs. Graham's
18     English class.
19  DRAKE: That essay that's due today?
20  JOHN: Yeah. But anyway, I'm trying to write my essay and
21     these zebra hamsters keep running across my paper
22     and pooping.
23  DRAKE: Yuck!
24  JOHN: And I'm trying to write, pushing away poop, pushing
25     away hamsters, pushing away more poop, and I'm
26     stressing! This assignment is due tomorrow.
27  DRAKE: Actually today. No less than twelve hundred words.
28  JOHN: But the hamsters, the poop. Everywhere! I can't write
29     with them scurrying all over my notebook paper.
30  DRAKE: And pooping all over your notebook paper!
31  JOHN: Forget the dog ate my homework.
32  DRAKE: "The hamsters pooped on my paper!" Is that what
33     you're going to tell Mrs. Graham?
34  JOHN: It's true!
35  DRAKE: I thought you said it was a dream.

1  JOHN: In my dream it was real.

2  DRAKE: Question: Do you have an essay to turn into English

3      class today?

4  JOHN: No.

5  DRAKE: And you're going to tell Mrs. Graham that zebra

6      hamsters invaded your room and kept you from doing

7      your homework? I can't wait to hear this.

8  JOHN: I was writing my essay when suddenly, on accident, I

9      fell asleep.

10  DRAKE: Oh yeah. That'll work. That'll get her sympathy and

11      understanding.

12  JOHN: All night long I tossed and turned.

13  DRAKE: But you didn't write your essay.

14  JOHN: And the dream lasted all night long. I was fighting off

15      the hamsters! "Get off my homework! Get off! Get off!"

16  DRAKE: Sounds convincing.

17  JOHN: "I'm trying to write! I have to write! I have so much to

18      say! Not five hundred words! Not twelve hundred

19      words, but thousands and thousands of words!"

20  DRAKE: Sure, she'll believe that from a guy who counts the

21      heading and "the end" toward the word count.

22  JOHN: "Get off! Get off my paper! Stop it! Stop pooping

23      everywhere!"

24  DRAKE: Look, I don't think this is going to work. Mrs.

25      Graham doesn't know that you don't have a dog, so just

26      stick to the old tried and true – the dog ate my

27      homework.

28  JOHN: No! Zebra hamsters pooped on my homework!

29  DRAKE: *(Pats his back.)* Well, good luck with that.

30  JOHN: It's true.

31  DRAKE: You said it was a dream.

32  JOHN: Well, it's true that I fell asleep and had a dream.

33  DRAKE: And Mrs. Graham is supposed to understand?

34  JOHN: She did understand.

35  DRAKE: You already told her?

1   **JOHN: Yep.**

2   **DRAKE: And she said it was OK that you didn't have an essay**

3       **to turn in?**

4   **JOHN: Well, kinda.**

5   **DRAKE: Just what exactly did she say?**

6   **JOHN: She said she appreciated my honesty.**

7   **DRAKE: Really?**

8   **JOHN: And since I was obviously struggling so much with**

9       **this assignment, I should get another chance to do it.**

10  **DRAKE: You're kidding, right?**

11  **JOHN: Mrs. Graham said that dreams could be very**

12      **revealing. Inner struggles that we are feeling.**

13      **Hamsters pooping on my essay ... it's all tied together.**

14  **DRAKE: Really?**

15  **JOHN: So she's giving me a second chance.**

16  **DRAKE: Unbelievable! That'd never work for me. Man, did I**

17      **ever tell you that I hate you?**

18  **JOHN: Oh, but I did leave out one part.**

19  **DRAKE: What? What part?**

20  **JOHN: About my second chance ...**

21  **DRAKE: Yeah?**

22  **JOHN: Starts in June. Summer school.**

23  **DRAKE: Wow. Now that's a nightmare!**

# 13. The Rose

CAST: (2M, 5F) ALEX, OLIVIA, HAILEY, MIA, KAYLEE,
NOAH, MRS. MITCHELL
PROPS: A single rose
SETTING: School hallway

1     *(At rise, OLIVIA enters and ALEX holds out a rose and*
2     *offers it to her.)*
3   **ALEX: For you!**
4   **OLIVIA: I don't forgive you.**
5   **ALEX: Olivia, what's it going to take?**
6   **OLIVIA: Nothing.**
7   **ALEX: If it took nothing then you'd forgive me without the**
8     **rose.**
9   **OLIVIA: Let me put it this way. There's nothing you can do**
10     **to get me to forgive you.**
11  **ALEX: Nothing?**
12  **OLIVIA: That's right, Alex.**
13  **ALEX:** *(Holds out the rose.)* **But —**
14  **OLIVIA: Keep your stupid rose!** *(She exits. HAILEY enters.*
15     *ALEX offers her the rose.)*
16  **ALEX: For you!**
17  **HAILEY: Why?**
18  **ALEX: Because I think you're beautiful.**
19  **HAILEY: Really?**
20  **ALEX: Really.**
21  **HAILEY: No.**
22  **ALEX: No?**
23  **HAILEY: Alex, the truth is you want me to give you those**
24     **answers to the one hundred questions that Mr.**
25     **Hawthorne handed out in science class yesterday.**
26     **Which is due tomorrow and knowing you, you haven't**
27     **even started on them. Am I right?**
28  **ALEX: No.**

1   HAILEY: No? So you don't want the answers to the one
2       hundred questions?
3   ALEX: Well, no ... I mean I do. *(Holding out the rose)* **Would**
4       you?
5   HAILEY: No.
6   ALEX: But —
7   HAILEY: No! I don't believe in cheating. And even if I were
8       kind enough to help you out in this one instance, you'd
9       just take my answers and run off to all of your dummy
10      friends and let them copy them as well. As if *you'd* done
11      all the work. And I'm not going to have any part of that.
12  ALEX: But Hailey, if I shared the answers with the guys,
13      they'd love me for it. And I'd give you half the credit.
14  HAILEY: Half the credit when I did all the work?
15  ALEX: I'll say it was a combined effort.
16  HAILEY: No!
17  ALEX: OK, Hailey. Fine! I'll say it was all you. I'll give you one
18      hundred percent of the credit. You and you alone.
19      *(Holds out the rose.)* **For a beautiful person.**
20  HAILEY: Forget it, Alex.
21  ALEX: But —
22  HAILEY: No! *(Exits. MIA enters. ALEX offers her the rose.)*
23  ALEX: For you.
24  MIA: Oh really? For me?
25  ALEX: For you and only you.
26  MIA: *(Takes the rose.)* **How sweet.**
27  ALEX: Thank you.
28  MIA: *(Smells the rose.)* **How sweet of you to remember**
29      Benji's death.
30  ALEX: Benji?
31  MIA: My dog that died four months ago. It's been all over
32      Facebook this week. I even set Benji's picture as my
33      profile picture.
34  ALEX: It was on Facebook?
35  MIA: You didn't see it?

1   ALEX: No.
2   MIA: Then how did you know?
3   ALEX: I didn't.
4   MIA: Then what's this for?
5   ALEX: For —
6   MIA: For what?
7   ALEX: Our friendship.
8   MIA: Really?
9   ALEX: Really!
10  MIA: What brought this on?
11  ALEX: You're just a special friend to me, Mia.
12  MIA: Oh. Well, thanks.
13  ALEX: You're welcome. Hey, I just thought of something I
14      wanted to ask you. Would you mind if I borrowed those
15      one hundred answers to the questions Mr. Hawthorne
16      handed out in science class yesterday? It's due
17      tomorrow and I haven't had a free second to work on
18      them. Please?
19  MIA: Borrow? Don't you mean copy?
20  ALEX: Borrow ... copy ... it's all the same thing. But yeah. If
21      you don't mind.
22  MIA: I do mind.
23  ALEX: But —
24  MIA: No.
25  ALEX: No?
26  MIA: No!
27  ALEX: Thanks for being a special friend, Mia! And hey, can I
28      have my rose back?
29  MIA: *(Hands him the rose.)* Sure! Some special friend you
30      are! *(Exits. KAYLEE enters. ALEX offers her the rose.)*
31  ALEX: For you.
32  KAYLEE: What'd you do? Steal that from Mrs. Mitchell's
33      vase on her desk? Thinking she wouldn't miss one rose
34      out of the dozen she received for her birthday.
35  ALEX: She won't miss it. *(Smiles.)* But it's for you.

1   KAYLEE: Unless I tell her.

2   ALEX: Kaylee, I want you to have it. You're the one who

3        deserves it.

4   KAYLEE: Like I'd want one of Mrs. Mitchell's stolen

5        birthday roses?

6   ALEX: It's the thought that counts, right?

7   KAYLEE: Not if it's stolen! And I think I'm going to tell Mrs.

8        Mitchell what you did.

9   ALEX: No, Kaylee! Don't do that.

10  KAYLEE: Yes! I think I'll tell Mrs. Mitchell that she should

11       count the roses in her vase. Then when she looks

12       surprised and confused, I'll just happen to mention

13       that I saw Alex Lujan walking around with a single

14       rose. Hmmmm ... Isn't that ironic?

15  ALEX: But Kaylee, I wanted you to have it. That's why I took

16       it.

17  KAYLEE: You wanted me to have it?

18  ALEX: Yes!

19  KAYLEE: Why?

20  ALEX: Because I wanted you to ...

21  KAYLEE: What?

22  ALEX: *(Suddenly)* To know that I love you!

23  KAYLEE: What? You love me?

24  ALEX: Confession time. I love you, Kaylee!

25  KAYLEE: Really?

26  ALEX: *(Offers her the rose.)* A rose for the love of my life.

27  KAYLEE: *(Hugs him.)* Alex!

28  ALEX: Yes?

29  KAYLEE: I didn't know! All this time you've been in love

30       with me?

31  ALEX: Yes! You and your superb intellectual mind.

32  KAYLEE: You think I'm smart?

33  ALEX: As smart as they come. I admire your smartness. Your

34       intellect. Your ability to find those answers to difficult

35       questions. And most of all, Kaylee, I love you even more

1 for it.

2 **KAYLEE:** *(Throws arms around ALEX.)* **Oh, Alex!**

3 **ALEX:** *(Pries her off.)* **And I bet you already finished those**
4 **one hundred answers to those one hundred questions**
5 **that Mr. Hawthorne handed out in science class**
6 **yesterday, didn't you?**

7 **KAYLEE: What one hundred questions?**

8 **ALEX: Those one hundred questions that Mr. Hawthorne**
9 **handed out in science class yesterday. Remember? It's**
10 **due tomorrow.**

11 **KAYLEE: Oh that! Finished that last night.**

12 **ALEX: So anyway, sweetheart, do you want to get together**
13 **after school?**

14 **KAYLEE: Really?**

15 **ALEX: Uh-huh. Maybe you could help me with my one**
16 **hundred questions ... that is since you're finished and**
17 **you're so much smarter than me. Did I tell you I like**
18 **smart women?**

19 **KAYLEE: You want me to help you with your one hundred**
20 **questions?**

21 **ALEX: If you don't mind, my love.**

22 **KAYLEE:** *(Sweetly)* **But I do mind. I'm so tired of homework.**
23 **So if you could rush home after school and finish those**
24 **questions, then maybe we could go to a movie or**
25 **something tonight.**

26 **ALEX: I'd love to, Kaylee ... my love ... but I'm such a dummy**
27 **compared to you. I'm afraid it'd take me all night long.**

28 **KAYLEE: Sweetheart, it's OK. I understand you have**
29 **homework that might keep you occupied all night. So,**
30 **we'll just plan on that movie this weekend. OK?**

31 **ALEX: Ah, forget it!** *(Starts to walk off, then turns and goes*
32 *back to her and takes back the rose.)*

33 **KAYLEE: Why did you take it back?**

34 **ALEX: Kaylee, it's over.**

35 **KAYLEE: It's over?**

1   ALEX: The love. It died.

2   KAYLEE: You jerk! You were just trying to get my answers to
3        those one hundred questions for Mr. Hawthorne's
4        class. You know what? I am going to go tell Mrs.
5        Mitchell to count the roses in her vase. *(Stomps off.)*

6   ALEX: Great! *(NOAH enters. ALEX offers him the rose.)*

7   ALEX: For you.

8   NOAH: *(Gives him a strange look.)* For me?

9   ALEX: Yes, Noah. It's for you. *(Looks around.)* Take it!

10  NOAH: *(Takes the rose.)* What is this?

11  ALEX: A rose.

12  NOAH: I know that. But why are you giving it to me?

13  ALEX: It's a gift.

14  NOAH: But ... this is weird. Creepy. Actually, it's wrong. Here,
15        you take it back. I don't want it.

16  ALEX: I can't take it back.

17  NOAH: Why not?

18  ALEX: Because it's yours. Noah, you shouldn't give back a
19        gift that someone has given to you.

20  NOAH: I know, but ... guys don't give other guys flowers.

21  ALEX: Why not?

22  NOAH: It's wrong. And like I said, it's creepy.

23  ALEX: Do you want to know what's wrong?

24  NOAH: What?

25  ALEX: I haven't finished those one hundred questions that
26        Mr. Hawthorne handed out in science class.

27  NOAH: Really? I did mine last night.

28  ALEX: Great! Hey buddy. *(Pats his back.)* Any chance you'd let
29        your friend here borrow those answers?

30  NOAH: Sure.

31  ALEX: Great!

32  NOAH: But there's just one little problem.

33  ALEX: What's that?

34  NOAH: I turned my paper in early. I won't be at school
35        tomorrow because I have a dentist appointment. Sorry.

1   **ALEX: Man! All this trouble for nothing.**

2   **NOAH: What do you mean?**

3   **ALEX: Nothing! Forget it. Hey, I've gotta run.**

4   **NOAH:** *(Holds out the rose.)* **But what about this?**

5   **ALEX: It's yours! Hope you enjoy it. Bye.** *(Quickly exits.)*

6   **MRS. MITCHELL:** *(Enters.)* **So it was you.**

7   **NOAH: Me?**

8   **MRS. MITCHELL:** *Yes, you!*

9   **NOAH:** *(Smiles, confused. Thinking quickly)* **Uh ... uh ... for**

10     **you!** *(Offers her the rose.)*

11   **MRS. MITCHELL: Oh, that's not going to work with me,**

12     **mister. Trying to be funny, are you?**

13   **NOAH: No, I ... I just wanted to give you this rose.**

14   **MRS. MITCHELL:** *(Grabs his shirt.)* **Look here, funny guy,**

15     **you stole that rose from the vase off my desk.**

16   **NOAH: I did?**

17   **MRS. MITCHELL: Yes, you did.**

18   **NOAH: No, I didn't!**

19   **MRS. MITCHELL: And you are in serious trouble. Let's go!**

20     *(Dragging him off)* **Stealing one of my birthday roses ...**

21     **Shame on you!**

22   **NOAH: But it wasn't me!**

23   **MRS. MITCHELL:** *(Stops. Mocking him)* **"But it wasn't me!"**

24     **And don't give me that line about someone else giving**

25     **it to you.**

26   **NOAH: But it's true. My friend just handed this rose to me.**

27   **MRS. MITCHELL:** *(Stops.)* **Who?**

28   **NOAH: Oh, never mind. You wouldn't believe me.**

29   **MRS. MITCHELL: What I do believe is that you stole my**

30     **rose.**

31   **NOAH: But ... if you'd just let me explain.**

32   **MRS. MITCHELL: And you'd say what? That you were trying**

33     **to give my birthday rose to some girl you were**

34     **desperately trying to impress? Handing it off to her as**

35     **if you'd bought it yourself?**

1   **NOAH: No.**

2   **MRS. MITCHELL: Because you thought you were in love and**

3       **you thought you had to present her with a rose?**

4   **NOAH: No.**

5   **MRS. MITCHELL: Because that's about the only reason you**

6       **could give me that would allow me to forgive you for**

7       **being a thief.** *(In a dreamy tone)* **A boy in love ...**

8       **desperate to give his love a rose.** *(Screams.)* **Is that it?!**

9   **NOAH: Yes! Yes! I'm in love, Mrs. Mitchell!**

10  **MRS. MITCHELL:** *(Not sure if to believe him)* **With whom?**

11      *(OLIVIA enters.)*

12  **NOAH:** *(Pointing)* **With her!**

13  **MRS. MITCHELL: Olivia, come over here please.**

14  **OLIVIA: Yes ma'am?**

15  **MRS. MITCHELL: Noah has something to tell you. Go ahead,**

16      **Noah.**

17  **NOAH:** *(To MRS. MITCHELL)* **I have to do this in front of you?**

18  **MRS. MITCHELL:** *(Smiles.)* **I don't mind. After all, it was my**

19      **you-know-what to begin with. So, go ahead.**

20  **NOAH: Olivia, I ... uh ...**

21  **OLIVIA: Yes?**

22  **NOAH: Uh ... I ... uh ...**

23  **OLIVIA: Yes?**

24  **NOAH: I ... uh ...** *(Hands her the rose.)* **For you!**

25  **OLIVIA: For me?**

26  **MRS. MITCHELL: He's in love with you, Olivia, and he's**

27      **afraid to tell you.**

28  **OLIVIA:** *(Looking at the rose)* **This is the same rose that Alex**

29      **tried to give me a little earlier. I didn't fall for his see-**

30      **through attempt to get homework out of me and I'm**

31      **not falling for whatever game you're playing either,**

32      **Noah.** *(Gives the rose back to NOAH.)* **So no! I don't want**

33      **this stupid rose.**

34  **MRS. MITCHELL: What?** *(Takes the rose from NOAH.)* **Alex**

35      **tried to give you this same rose?**

1   **OLIVIA: That's the one. And the reason I know it's the same**
2      **rose is because this petal is torn a bit. Probably by Alex!**
3   **MRS. MITCHELL:** *(To NOAH)* **So Alex handed this off to you**
4      **so he wouldn't get caught?**
5   **NOAH: That's what I was trying to tell you, but you wouldn't**
6      **listen to me.**
7   **MRS. MICHELL: And you're not in love with Olivia?**
8   **OLIVIA: What?**
9   **NOAH: No, I ...** *(Looks at OLIVIA. Suddenly in a dreamy tone)*
10     **Well, maybe. Yes, maybe I am ...**
11   **MRS. MITCHELL:** *(Hands the rose to NOAH.)* **Here. Keep it.**
12     **And good luck.** *(As she exits.)* **And I'm going to go find**
13     **Mr. Alex Lujan. I believe we need to have a little talk!**
14   **NOAH:** *(Smiling at OLIVIA, he holds the rose out to her.)* **For**
15     **you!** *(OLIVIA shakes her head and exits.)*

# 14. The Perfect Monologue

CAST: (2F) ANNA, CLAIRE
PROPS: Play scripts, monologue books
SETTING: Drama classroom

1  *(At rise, CLAIRE is sitting at a table surrounded by play*
2  *scripts and monologue books looking for a monologue to*
3  *use. As ANNA enters, CLAIRE slams a book shut.)*
4  ANNA: Claire, what's wrong?
5  CLAIRE: I can't find a monologue.
6  ANNA: You haven't found one yet?
7  CLAIRE: No! I keep searching and searching but I just can't
8      find the perfect monologue.
9  ANNA: I hate to remind you of this, but we have to perform
10     our monologues tomorrow.
11 CLAIRE: I know. Believe me, I know.
12 ANNA: I've already memorized mine. It took me a week.
13 CLAIRE: Oh, what am I going to do?
14 ANNA: Well, I say you just pick one and go with it.
15 CLAIRE: Sure. *(Opens book.)* How about this one, "My
16     Sister's Dying Wish"? *(Reads.)* "My sister cries herself to
17     sleep each night. She longs to see her mother. Our
18     mother. Our mother who abandoned us at the age of
19     three ... " I'm not memorizing this. It's too depressing.
20 ANNA: Let me help you look for something else. How about
21     this one, "My Four-Legged Friend"?
22 CLAIRE: A monologue about me talking to a dog? No thank
23     you.
24 ANNA: But it'd be cute. *(Reads.)* "'Max, sit!' I would tell him.
25     And Max would do just the opposite. He'd pick up his
26     red ball, run back to me, and put it at my feet. He didn't
27     want to sit. He wanted to play. 'Arf, arf, arf,' he'd say."

1   CLAIRE: No! Absolutely not. I'm not barking in front of my
2       peers.
3   ANNA: OK. Moving right along. "Teacher's Pet"?
4   CLAIRE: If I was ten years old.
5   ANNA: "The Mysteries of a Teen Mind?"
6   CLAIRE: Hasn't everyone done that one?
7   ANNA: "First Kiss"? *(Reading)* "My lips began to quiver a bit
8       as he moved in closer. I closed my eyes and thought, 'Is
9       this really about to happen?' So in anticipation, with
10     my eyes shut tight, I puckered my lips ... "
11   CLAIRE: No way am I doing that.
12   ANNA: Don't give up. There are plenty here to choose from.
13   CLAIRE: But I've looked at so many. Nothing is really
14     speaking to me. You know, I want to feel it. I want to be
15     able to climb inside my character's head and figure her
16     out. What troubles her? What are her strengths? Her
17     weaknesses? Because then, my performance will be
18     delivered with true feeling and emotion. But barking
19     like a dog or puckering my lips is not going to work for
20     me.
21   ANNA: Let's keep looking. *(Thumbing through the books)*
22     How about this one, "Searching for my Mother"?
23   CLAIRE: Another one everyone has done. Abandonment.
24     Discovery. Shock. Tears. It's depressing.
25   ANNA: Then let's look for a comedy. *(Flips through the*
26     *pages.)* "The Clumsy Ballerina"?
27   CLAIRE: No.
28   ANNA: "I Still Believe in the Tooth Fairy"?
29   CLAIRE: No.
30   ANNA: "Sleepwalking"?
31   CLAIRE: I saw Bethany do that last year. It was dumb.
32   ANNA: Yeah. *(Arms outstretched.)* Walking in place with a
33     sleepy look, her arms outstretched.
34   CLAIRE: *(Arms outstretched.)* I'm asleep, but I don't know it.
35   ANNA: I'm walking on the train tracks now.

1 CLAIRE: But in my mind, well my dream, I'm on a tropical
2     island.
3 ANNA: The warm sand under my feet.
4 CLAIRE: The sounds of the ocean.
5 ANNA: But in reality, the train is blaring its horn.
6 CLAIRE: But I don't hear it.
7 ANNA: I only hear the waves of the ocean.
8 CLAIRE: I never saw the train coming.
9 ANNA: And I die in my sleep.
10 CLAIRE: Actually, I die on the train tracks. In my sleep.
11 ANNA: That was a bad dream.
12 CLAIRE: And a bad monologue. It was supposed to be a
13     drama, but all of the students kept laughing at
14     Bethany. She looked like Frankenstein standing there
15     with her arms outstretched as she walked in place.
16 ANNA: Yeah, that was funny.
17 CLAIRE: Anna, I'll never find the perfect monologue.
18 ANNA: Or you're just too picky.
19 CLAIRE: No, I just want a good monologue. I want to be able
20     to connect with the character in the monologue. Not
21     stand on the stage and bark like a dog or act as if I'm
22     sleepwalking before an oncoming train kills me.
23 ANNA: I think I connect with my character.
24 CLAIRE: What are you doing?
25 ANNA: Macbeth.
26 CLAIRE: That role's for a guy.
27 ANNA: So? I like it. (*Demonstrates, dramatically.*) "Is this a
28     dagger, which I see before me? The handle toward my
29     hand? Come, let me clutch thee!"
30 CLAIRE: Did you tell Mr. Wilson you were doing Macbeth?
31 ANNA: He approved it. (*Continues.*) "I have thee not, and yet
32     I see thee still. Art thou not, fatal vision, sensible to
33     feeling as to sight? Or art thou but a dagger of the mind,
34     a false creation ... "
35 CLAIRE: Maybe I should steal your idea and do that one, too.

1 ANNA: No! I want to be original.
2 CLAIRE: You can't be original with Shakespeare.
3 ANNA: I mean the only one in our class doing Macbeth.
4 CLAIRE: Fine. I'll find something else. Hopefully.
5 ANNA: Well, you better do it fast because you still have to
6     memorize yours. In one day, if I might add.
7 CLAIRE: How about this one? "The Voices in my Head."
8 ANNA: It sounds a little dark, but let me hear some of it.
9 CLAIRE: *(Dramatically)* "The voices in my head are growing
10     louder and louder and I don't know how much more of
11     this I can take. The constant sounds. The screaming.
12     What are they saying? What are they telling me to do? I
13     don't understand. 'Get out of my head,' I say. But the
14     voices refuse to leave. What? What was that? Mother?
15     *(Looks around.)* I hear you, but ... you're not here. What?
16     Who is this? Who is saying these things? Who are you?
17     Go away! You're my enemy! What are you saying?
18     You're telling me to jump? *(Grabs her head.)* Stop it!
19     Stop! I won't! I won't do it! Mother? Where are you? I
20     hear you, but ... I know you're not here. You blame me?
21     For what? But that was an accident. I didn't know the
22     candle was too close to the towels. You'll never forgive
23     me? But I'm sorry!"
24 ANNA: Sounds like someone needs to seek counseling.
25 CLAIRE: *(Ignores her, continues.)* "Who is that talking to
26     me?"
27 ANNA: Maybe some medication would help, too
28 CLAIRE: *(Continues.)* "What? What did you say?"
29 ANNA: I said maybe your character needs some medication.
30     To quiet those voices.
31 CLAIRE: "You said I could fly. Do you mean it? Then maybe
32     ... maybe I can." *(Raises her arms.)* "Yes! I believe I can
33     fly!"
34 ANNA: Don't do it.
35 CLAIRE: *(Looks at ANNA.)* What? Fly or do this monologue?

1 ANNA: Either. It sounds like a downer.

2 CLAIRE: How can you say anything when you're doing
3    Macbeth? "Is this a dagger, in front of me? Let me
4    clutch it and ... " *(As if stabbing herself)*

5 ANNA: That's not how it goes! And that's Shakespeare. You
6    can't knock Shakespeare. He's considered the greatest
7    writer in world history.

8 CLAIRE: Well, you can't knock this author either.

9 ANNA: Who wrote it?

10 CLAIRE: *(Looks at the playbook.)* Anonymous.

11 ANNA: *(Laughs.)* "The Voices in My Head," by Anonymous?

12 CLAIRE: I like it!

13 ANNA: Then you better get it approved and start
14    memorizing it. And fast.

15 CLAIRE: It'll be a cinch. I've already got the first several
16    lines in my head.

17 ANNA: I'm not sure that's a good thing. Are they talking to
18    you?

19 CLAIRE: *(Dramatically)* "The voices in my head are growing
20    louder and louder and I don't know how much more of
21    this I can take. The constant sounds. The screaming.
22    What are they saying?"

23 ANNA: Maybe they're saying to pick another monologue.

24 CLAIRE: *(Looks at ANNA.)* Oh, go work on your own
25    monologue.

26 ANNA: Actually, I believe I will. *(Dramatically)* "I go, and it is
27    done. The bell invites me. Hear it not, Duncan, for it is a
28    knell, that summons thee to heaven, or to hell." *(She exits.)*

29 CLAIRE: *(Looking at the script)* "What? What are you saying
30    to me? Stop screaming! I can't understand you when
31    you scream! But I'm not a bird! I'm afraid to fly! No, I
32    can't! I don't know how! What? Just take one step
33    forward? But ... All right. I will." *(Steps forward, then
34    falls to the ground. After a moment, she looks up and
35    smiles.)* The end.

# 15. Roadside Cleanup

CAST: (1M, 3F) SYDNEY, ALISSA, KATIE, MR. LATHAM
PROPS: Trash bags, gloves, lottery ticket, empty Coke can,
newspaper, penny, broken toy, chicken bone, plastic
sacks, empty water bottle, book report, dirty rag, straw,
paper cup, hairpiece or wig, and any other various items
of trash for the girls to pick up
SETTING: The roadside of a highway

1  (At rise, the GIRLS are each wearing gloves, holding trash
2  bags, and picking up trash from the ground.)
3  SYDNEY: I'm tired of picking up trash off the side of the
4  road.
5  ALISSA: Me too. And we've only been out here for ten minutes.
6  KATIE: Who signed us up for this, anyway?
7  SYDNEY: We were forced to sign up, remember?
8  KATIE: Only because we needed that extra hundred points
9  for Mr. Latham's geometry class. The naming polygons
10  did me in. I did OK up to the hexagon, but after that, I
11  was lost.
12  SYDNEY: Yeah, well I had issues with longitude and
13  latitude.
14  ALISSA: I had problems with all of it. I'm two points away
15  from passing his class.
16  SYDNEY: So here we are at seven a.m. on Saturday morning.
17  KATIE: Picking up trash.
18  ALISSA: Making our city beautiful again. More importantly,
19  getting that extra hundred points!
20  KATIE: People should pick up their own trash.
21  SYDNEY: This wind is getting on my nerves.
22  ALISSA: I know. I hate the wind.
23  KATIE: Glad I put my hair in a ponytail.
24  SYDNEY: Where did all this stuff come from?
25  ALISSA: Some of it was probably thrown out of car
26  windows.

1   KATIE: True. The rest of it probably just blew this way.
2       Especially with the horrible wind we've been having
3       lately.
4   SYDNEY: Here's a lottery ticket. *(Drops it in the trash bag.)*
5       Guess it wasn't a winner.
6   ALISSA: *(Looking at an empty Coke can)* Do you know how
7       many calories are in a Coke? One hundred and five.
8       And zero grams of fat.
9   SYDNEY: I could use a Coke right now.
10  KATIE: Me too. How long have we been at this?
11  SYDNEY: *(Looks at watch.)* About twelve minutes.
12  KATIE: That's all? It feels like forever.
13  ALISSA: Forever and a day.
14  KATIE: When does this end?
15  SYDNEY: When it's all cleaned up or at noon. Whichever
16      comes first.
17  KATIE: All this work for a stupid hundred points.
18  ALISSA: Yeah, but I desperately need that hundred points.
19  SYDNEY: I think we all do. Do you hear that? Mr. Latham is
20      screaming at us.
21  ALISSA: What did he say?
22  SYDNEY: He said pick it up a notch.
23  KATIE: Guess we better. *(ALL pick up trash.)*
24  SYDNEY: Guess Mr. Latham is proud of himself for letting
25      his math class adopt a highway.
26  ALISSA: I'd rather adopt a kitten and take care of it.
27  SYDNEY: And once a month, rain or shine, you have the
28      privilege of slaving away for an extra one hundred
29      points.
30  KATIE: And as hard as Mr. Latham's class is, it's no wonder
31      most of his students are scattered about this two-mile
32      stretch of highway picking up trash.
33  ALISSA: I'm already tired.
34  SYDNEY: Me too.
35  ALISSA: *(Looks inside a newspaper.)* Oh my gosh! There's a

1    **dirty diaper inside this newspaper.**
2  **KATIE: Yuck!**
3  **SYDNEY: Hey, I found a penny.**
4  **KATIE: That'll buy a lot.**
5  **SYDNEY: I'm keeping it. Maybe it'll bring me good luck.**
6  **ALISSA: Here's a broken toy.**
7  **KATIE: And lots of crumpled up paper. This one's a receipt.**
8  *(Looks at it.)* **Let's see, this person bought bread,**
9  **bananas, cat food, eggplant, chips, beer, taco seasoning**
10  **mix, hot sauce, cheese, macaroni and cheese –**
11  **SYDNEY: Just throw it away, Katie. It's really not that**
12  **exciting.**
13  **ALISSA: Here's a nasty chicken bone.**
14  **KATIE: And another plastic bag.**
15  **SYDNEY: Sack of leftover food. Anyone want some stale**
16  **French fries?**
17  **ALISSA: I'll pass.**
18  **KATIE: Me too. Do we have to pick up dog poop?**
19  **ALISSA: I'm not.**
20  **SYDNEY: Me either.**
21  **KATIE: Here's a book report.** *(Reading)* **Uncle Tom's Cabin**
22  **by Harriet Beecher Stowe is the most powerful literary**
23  **achievement of American literature.**
24  **ALISSA: What'd they make?**
25  **SYDNEY: Yeah, maybe we can recycle it.**
26  **KATIE: They got a sixty-two.**
27  **SYDNEY: Hey, with a little polishing up, maybe one of us**
28  **could use it in the future.**
29  **KATIE: So I should keep it?**
30  **SYDNEY: I would.**
31  **KATIE:** *(Folds it up and puts in her pocket.)* **Saved for a rainy**
32  **day.**
33  **ALISSA: I'm getting hungry.**
34  **SYDNEY: I have some old French fries.**
35  **ALISSA: No thanks! And another plastic bag.**

1　KATIE: Got one of those here, too.

2　SYDNEY: A dirty rag.

3　KATIE: Some sort of plastic thingamajig.

4　ALISSA: Another plastic bag.

5　SYDNEY: A straw.

6　KATIE: Paper cup.

7　ALISSA: Another plastic bag.

8　KATIE: Crumpled paper.

9　SYDNEY: Another book report?

10　KATIE: *(Opens the paper.)* A letter.

11　ALISSA: Read it.

12　KATIE: Dear Mr. Latham —

13　ALISSA: Mr. Latham?

14　SYDNEY: Our Mr. Latham?

15　ALISSA: I don't know, but this is his adopt-a-highway

16　　　　section. Maybe one of his students wrote him a letter

17　　　　then backed out of giving it to him.

18　SYDNEY: Read it, Katie.

19　KATIE: *(Reading)* Dear Mr. Latham, everyone in class knows

20　　　　that you wear a toupee —

21　ALISSA: What's a toupee?

22　SYDNEY: A hairpiece.

23　ALISSA: A wig? Mr. Latham wears a wig?

24　KATIE: *(Reading)* And while we were picking up trash we

25　　　　took a poll. Eighty-five percent of us think you'd look

26　　　　better bald. So here's a suggestion. Take it off, Mr.

27　　　　Latham. Because some days, it looks a little crooked on

28　　　　your head. You may not realize this, but it does.

29　MR. LATHAM: *(Enters.)* Having fun? *(GIRLS jump.)*

30　KATIE: *(Quickly crumples the paper)* Just picking up lots of

31　　　　trash, Mr. Latham!

32　ALISSA: Look at my bag. It's almost full.

33　SYDNEY: Mine too.

34　MR. LATHAM: What were you reading, Miss Smith?

35　KATIE: A ... uh ... book report. It was bad. They only got a

1    sixty-two on it.
2   MR. LATHAM: Are we out here to read book reports, Miss
3      Smith?
4   KATIE: No sir! Throwing it away.
5   MR. LATHAM: Let me see that.
6   KATIE: *(Drops it in the trash bag.)* Oh, sorry. I already threw
7      it away. But I can tell you what it was about. It was a
8      book report on *Uncle Tom's Cabin.* And it was bad. Talk
9      about missing the mark on one of the greatest novels in
10      American literature!
11   MR. LATHAM: Take it out and let me see it.
12   KATIE: OK. *(Digs around the bag.)* If I can find it ...
13   MR. LATHAM: It'll be on top, Miss Smith.
14   KATIE: Where is it? Silly thing disappeared. *(Still digging)*
15      And why would you want to read a failing book report?
16   MR. LATHAM: Because I don't believe that was a book
17      report. I believe it was something else.
18   KATIE: I'm sorry Mr. Latham, but I can't find it. It must have
19      somehow dropped to the bottom of my bag.
20   MR. LATHAM: Give me that! *(Grabs the bag and takes out the
21      letter and reads. The GIRLS nervously look at each other.
22      He crumples it up.)* Did you write this?
23   KATIE: No! I found it. I swear!
24   SYDNEY: I saw her pick it up from the ground, Mr. Latham.
25   ALISSA: Me too!
26   MR. LATHAM: *(Looks around, then touches his hair.)* And the
27      two of you were watching everything Miss Smith
28      picked up?
29   SYDNEY: No, we, uh ...
30   ALISSA: We're just picking stuff up together. And talking.
31      You know?
32   MR. LATHAM: All talking about this letter? *(They shake their
33      heads. He looks at KATIE.)* Did you show this to anyone
34      or read it out loud?
35   KATIE: I ... uh ... maybe.

1    **MR. LATHAM: Never mind. It doesn't matter. It's just a**
2        **bunch of lies, that's what it is.** *(Puts the crumpled letter*
3        *in his pocket.)* **Now all of you get back to work if you**
4        **want that extra hundred points!** *(Suddenly turns nice.)*
5        **Oh, and I have an idea. If we can all forget about that**
6        **letter of lies, I might accidentally give each one of you**
7        **an additional hundred points. Besides the one you're**
8        **getting for picking up trash. How would you like that?**
9    **ALISSA: I would love that, Mr. Latham, because I really need**
10       **the extra points.**
11   **MR. LATHAM: Yes you do.**
12   **SYDNEY: That whole thing works for me, too.**
13   **KATIE: But Mr. Latham, you don't have too.**
14   **ALISSA: Katie!**
15   **KATIE: But I mean, we'd really appreciate it!**
16   **MR. LATHAM:** *(Pulls the letter out of his pocket.)* **If this**
17       **remains our secret, and I mean it goes nowhere besides**
18       **a big black trash bag, then an extra hundred points will**
19       **be awarded to the three of you. Deal?**
20   **GIRLS: Yes sir!**
21   **MR. LATHAM:** *(Puts his hand on top of his head to make sure*
22       *everything is in place.)* **Stupid wind!** *(Screams.)* **Now get**
23       **back to work!** *(The GIRLS start picking up trash, not*
24       *saying a word. After a minute, a wig or hairpiece flies*
25       *through the air and lands where the GIRLS are picking*
26       *up trash. One of the GIRLS picks up the hairpiece. She*
27       *looks to the other GIRLS for guidance, but they shrug.*
28       *Quickly she throws it away, then they continue picking*
29       *up trash.)*
30   **KATIE: I didn't see a thing.**
31   **ALISSA: Me either.**
32   **SYDNEY: Stupid wind.**

# 16. Prom Date

CAST: (1M, 2F) CHLOE, BRIANNA, JONATHAN
PROPS: Cell phone
SETTING: School cafeteria

1     *(At rise, BRIANNA and CHLOE sit at a table in the*
2     *cafeteria. BRIANNA is sending a text on her cell phone.)*
3   CHLOE: What are you doing?
4   BRIANNA: Texting Jonathan.
5   CHLOE: Why? He's sitting right over there.
6   BRIANNA: Because I'm not talking to him.
7   CHLOE: But you're texting him?
8   BRIANNA: Only to tell him that I hate his guts. *(As she*
9     *finishes)* That felt good.
10  CHLOE: Brianna, why do you hate his guts?
11  BRIANNA: *(Looking at her phone)* Look! He said, "Good,
12     because I hate your guts, too." Now what am I supposed
13     to say?
14  CHLOE: I don't know. Say, "I hate your guts more."
15  BRIANNA: Yeah! *(Sends a text message.)*
16  CHLOE: Why?
17  BRIANNA: Why?
18  CHLOE: Why do you hate his guts?
19  BRIANNA: Because he's an idiot.
20  CHLOE: Since?
21  BRIANNA: Since he told me he was inviting you to the prom.
22  CHLOE: Whoa! He said what?
23  BRIANNA: He said he was inviting you to the prom. *(Looking*
24     *at her phone)* Look! He said, "Not possible because the
25     extent of my hate towards you extends to the outer
26     universe."
27  CHLOE: Jonathan didn't ask me to the prom.
28  BRIANNA: He's going to. So what am I supposed to say now?
29  CHLOE: Excuse me! What am *I* supposed to say?

1   BRIANNA: I'll say ... let's see ... I know! *(Texting)* "The extent
2      of my hate for you is beyond your imagination!"
3   CHLOE: You hate him for asking me to the prom?
4   BRIANNA: I hate him because we already had plans to go
5      together.
6   CHLOE: You did?
7   BRIANNA: Yes, we did! Three weeks ago I told him we
8      should hook up and go to the prom together since
9      neither of us had a date.
10  CHLOE: And what did Jonathan say?
11  BRIANNA: He said, "Yeah." So "yeah" to me is like yes. It was
12      set. We were going to the prom together.
13  CHLOE: Well, I guess he wanted to go with someone else.
14  BRIANNA: You! *(Looks at her phone.)* Look what he said!
15      "Whatever!" I hate that comeback, don't you?
16      Whatever. So what am I supposed to say now?
17  CHLOE: I don't know.
18  BRIANNA: *(Texting)* I'll just say whatever, too.
19  CHLOE: I have a better idea.
20  BRIANNA: What?
21  CHLOE: Let's talk to Jonathan and see what's going on. You
22      know, face to face.
23  BRIANNA: No! I'm never speaking to him again. And you
24      know what's sad?
25  CHLOE: What?
26  BRIANNA: Last week, I bought my prom dress.
27  CHLOE: On a "yeah"?
28  BRIANNA: I told you I thought his "yeah" meant "yes."
29      Doesn't it sound like a yes to you?
30  CHLOE: Maybe. *(Motions.)* Hey, Jonathan, come over here.
31  BRIANNA: Stop it! Don't do that.
32  CHLOE: Here he comes.
33  JONATHAN: *(Enters.)* Hey.
34  CHLOE: Hey, Jonathan.
35  JONATHAN: Listen Chloe, there was something I wanted to

1      ask you.
2   BRIANNA: You're going to do this in front of me? OK, that's
3      fine. Don't mind me. Pretend I'm not here.
4   JONATHAN: Chloe, I was wondering —
5   CHLOE: Wait! Before you ask me anything, I need to tell you
6      both that I already have a date to the prom.
7   JONATHAN: You do?
8   BRIANNA: You do? *(Smiles. Looks at JONATHAN.)* Ahhhh ...
9      too bad for you.
10  CHLOE: *(Looks at watch.)* Sorry guys, but I've gotta run. I
11     promised to meet Katie in the band hall. Talk to you
12     later. *(She exits.)*
13  JONATHAN: So, Brianna, do you want to ...
14  BRIANNA: What?
15  JONATHAN: Want to forget that I hate you to the extent of
16     the entire universe?
17  BRIANNA: Not really.
18  JONATHAN: OK.
19  BRIANNA: Do you?
20  JONATHAN: Not really.
21  BRIANNA: And why would I, anyway? *(They yell back and
22     forth as they speak.)*
23  JONATHAN: I don't know, but you started this whole fight!
24  BRIANNA: How?
25  JONATHAN: With the whole I-hate-your-guts thing!
26  BRIANNA: Because Blake told me you were asking Chloe to
27     the prom when you already had a date with me! Or did
28     you forget that?
29  JONATHAN: We had a date?
30  BRIANNA: Were you asleep when I suggested we hook up
31     and go to the prom together?
32  JONATHAN: No!
33  BRIANNA: Then why did you say, "Yeah"?
34  JONATHAN: I thought that you meant we should hook up ...
35     as in meet up ... like double date. You and your date and

1    me and my date.

2    **BRIANNA: That's what you thought I meant?**

3    **JONATHAN: That's what I thought you meant! But we can't**

4        **do that now because I don't have a date.**

5    **BRIANNA: Well, neither do I.**

6    **JONATHAN: Then maybe we should hook up and go**

7        **together.**

8    **BRIANNA: Maybe so.**

9    **JONATHAN: So do you want to go with me to the prom?**

10   **BRIANNA: Yes.**

11   **JONATHAN: OK, fine.**

12   **BRIANNA: Fine!**

13   **JONATHAN: Then I'll pick you up at seven on Saturday!**

14   **BRIANNA: Fine!**

15   **JONATHAN:** *(Points to his wrist.)* **And what color of that thing**

16       **that you wear right here should I get you?**

17   **BRIANNA: Red. And I'll get you a red thing for here, too!**

18       *(Points to her chest.)*

19   **JONATHAN: Fine! So text me later.**

20   **BRIANNA: OK! I will!**

21   **JONATHAN: OK! Bye!**

22   **BRIANNA: Bye!** *(They each exit in opposite directions.*

23       *BRIANNA stops on one end of the stage to send him a*

24       *text.)* **"I think we'll have a great time."**

25   **JONATHAN:** *(Stops on the opposite end of the stage to text*

26       *BRIANNA.)* **"Me too."**

27   **BRIANNA:** *(Texting)* **"And don't forget, red."**

28   **JONATHAN:** *(Texting)* **"I won't. See you at seven."**

29   **BRIANNA:** *(Texting)* **"Perfect."**

# 17. Big Fat Liar

CAST: (2M) TYLER, LOGAN
SETTING: School hallway

1   **TYLER: Logan, what's wrong with you today? Did your pet**
2     **goldfish die?**
3   **LOGAN: I don't have a goldfish.**
4   **TYLER: Did Jaci dump you for someone else?**
5   **LOGAN: Jaci and I are fine.**
6   **TYLER: Then what?**
7   **LOGAN:** *(Shakes head.)* **I don't know if I can talk about it.**
8   **TYLER: Come on, Logan. I'm your friend. You can talk to me**
9     **about anything. And it sounds like you need to get**
10   **something off your chest. So what's wrong?**
11   **LOGAN: It's my mom.**
12   **TYLER: Is she OK?**
13   **LOGAN: She's OK. It's just what I did.**
14   **TYLER: To your mom?**
15   **LOGAN: Yes. Tyler, I lied.**
16   **TYLER: You lied to your mom? So?**
17   **LOGAN: And I'm feeling really guilty about it. I mean, the**
18   **guilt is eating me alive.**
19   **TYLER: You're kidding, right?**
20   **LOGAN: No, Tyler. I'm not kidding. I'm a liar. A big fat liar!**
21   **TYLER: So, what did you lie about?**
22   **LOGAN: The strawberry cheesecake.**
23   **TYLER:** *(Giving him a strange look)* **You lied about**
24   **strawberry cheesecake and it's killing you?**
25   **LOGAN: Yes! Yes it is!**
26   **TYLER: And you lied about it because ... ?**
27   **LOGAN: I wanted to eat it. So not only am I a big fat liar, I'm**
28   **an overeater as well. Maybe I should go to Overeaters**
29   **Anonymous.**

1   TYLER: I'm sorry, but I don't get it. Was the cheesecake
2       sacred at your house or something?
3   LOGAN: Yes it is ... or was, that is. But it's gone now. *(Cries.)*
4       Because I ate it all. All of it!
5   TYLER: Logan, I'm still a bit confused. Let's start from the
6       beginning. There was a strawberry cheesecake in the
7       refrigerator, right?
8   LOGAN: Right. There was. *(Cries.)* But it's gone now!
9   TYLER: OK, OK, calm down. But you're telling me that the
10      strawberry cheesecake was off limits, correct?
11  LOGAN: Yes. It was off limits, but I ... well, you know what I
12      did.
13  TYLER: And tell me, Logan, why was the cheesecake off
14      limits?
15  LOGAN: Because it was for my mom's Bunco party. She was
16      going to serve it to the women who were coming over
17      tonight.
18  TYLER: And you opened the fridge and ...
19  LOGAN: Became mesmerized by the strawberry
20      cheesecake. My mouth started watering and I thought
21      if I could just have one little bite ... Then one bite
22      turned into a sliver and the sliver turned into a huge
23      piece and the next thing I knew ... *(Cries.)* Oh, what have
24      I done?
25  TYLER: We'll figure this out, Logan. Pull yourself together.
26  LOGAN: *(Grabs TYLER's shoulder for support.)* I couldn't
27      help myself, Tyler! Strawberry cheesecake is my
28      weakness.
29  TYLER: So what happened when your mom noticed that her
30      cheesecake had disappeared from the fridge?
31  LOGAN: She screamed at me. "Logan, did you eat my
32      cheesecake?"
33  TYLER: And what did you say?
34  LOGAN: I said, "What cheesecake?"
35  TYLER: Good answer. Then what did she say?

1　LOGAN: Then she said, "What cheesecake? The cheesecake
2　　　that I slaved over all morning for my party!"
3　TYLER: And you said?
4　LOGAN: *(Casually)* "Nope, haven't seen it." Lied straight to
5　　　her face.
6　TYLER: I don't see a problem here, but OK. Then what?
7　LOGAN: Then Mom went a little mad.
8　TYLER: Uh-oh.
9　LOGAN: She started searching the entire house for the
10　　　cheesecake. She looked everywhere. And I mean
11　　　everywhere! In all the cabinets, the closets, under the
12　　　beds ...
13　TYLER: Under the beds?
14　LOGAN: Yeah. And Mom was saying, "Have I lost my mind?
15　　　Did I just think I put the cheesecake in the refrigerator
16　　　but I actually put it somewhere else?" Then she started
17　　　crying.
18　TYLER: Uh-oh.
19　LOGAN: I was like, "Mom, don't cry. It was just a
20　　　cheesecake."
21　TYLER: I bet that was the wrong thing to say.
22　LOGAN: It sure was. Then she started screaming at me. "It
23　　　wasn't just a cheesecake! It was the dessert for my
24　　　Bunco party. And now what am I going to do? Whip out
25　　　some potato chips and celery sticks? I just want to
26　　　know what happened to my cheesecake!"
27　TYLER: Wow. Sounds like she was going nuts over the
28　　　cheesecake.
29　LOGAN: Then I made the mistake of trying to make a joke
30　　　out of it.
31　TYLER: Uh-oh.
32　LOGAN: I said, "Well, maybe it grew legs and walked off."
33　TYLER: I bet that didn't go over well.
34　LOGAN: You're right about that. Because then she started
35　　　screaming and throwing utensils all over the kitchen. A

1       spatula, beater, cheese grater, measuring cup ... all

2       flying past my head. I had to duck and jump out of the

3       way the entire time. I pleaded with her to stop, but she

4       wouldn't.

5 TYLER: I'm wondering, at that point why didn't you just go

6       ahead and admit that you had eaten the cheesecake?

7 LOGAN: With her acting like that? Throwing spatulas and

8       wooden spoons?

9 TYLER: Logan, are you actually afraid of a wooden spoon?

10 LOGAN: I am when it's in my mom's right hand. *(Rubs his*

11       *behind.)* Man, I remember that wooden spoon.

12 TYLER: So you lied.

13 LOGAN: Yes. I lied. I devoured the entire strawberry

14       cheesecake in less than ten minutes.

15 TYLER: Wow.

16 LOGAN: And now ... now ... *(Begins to cry again.)* The guilt is

17       killing me!

18 TYLER: Sure it's not your stomach that's killing you from

19       eating an entire cheesecake?

20 LOGAN: No! I lied to my mom. I ruined her party! She's

21       upset. *(Crying)* And now I'm upset.

22 TYLER: So actually, eating the strawberry cheesecake

23       wasn't worth it considering all the pain and suffering

24       you caused your mother over this selfish indulgence.

25 LOGAN: Well, I wouldn't exactly say that. It was good. I

26       mean, it was awesome! I mean, maybe it was worth it.

27       Like I said, strawberry cheesecake is my weakness.

28 TYLER: There you have it. And life goes on.

29 LOGAN: No! I must confess.

30 TYLER: Are you sure about that?

31 LOGAN: Yes! I must. This guilt is going to wear me down. I

32       can't live with myself knowing what I've done.

33 TYLER: Which means the consequences of your actions

34       await you. Wonder what that'll be?

35 LOGAN: Knowing how upset my mom was, I'll probably be

1   grounded for life.
2   **TYLER:** Or ...
3   **LOGAN:** Or what?
4   **TYLER:** That wooden spoon.
5   **LOGAN:** You're right. Ouch!
6   **TYLER:** Good luck.
7   **LOGAN:** Thanks. I'm going to need it!

# 18. Fender Bender

CAST: (3M, 2F) ALICIA, AUSTIN, JESSICA, CARLOS, LUIS
PROPS: Store shopping bags
SETTING: Parking lot

1    *(At rise, ALICIA rushes to AUSTIN.)*

2    **ALICIA:** Did you not see me?

3    **AUSTIN:** Not see you? Did you not see me?

4    **ALICIA:** You're the one who hit me!

5    **AUSTIN:** I didn't hit you. You hit me!

6    **ALICIA:** No I didn't. You hit me!

7    **JESSICA:** *(Enters.)* Excuse me, I was in the car with Alicia
8       and I saw the whole thing.

9    **AUSTIN:** Good! So who hit who?

10    **JESSICA:** *(To AUSTIN)* You hit her.

11    **ALICIA:** See. Jessica and I both looked back and saw that it
12      was all clear. Right, Jessica?

13    **JESSICA:** That's right.

14    **ALICIA:** So slowly and carefully I began to back up when
15      *wham!*

16    **JESSICA:** *(Rubbing her neck)* I think I might have whiplash.

17    **CARLOS:** *(Enters.)* Austin, which one of these girls hit your
18      car? Man I was looking at the damage. *(Shakes head.)*
19      It's not pretty. Not pretty at all.

20    **JESSICA:** Your friend Austin is the one who hit my friend's
21      car.

22    **CARLOS:** That's not true. Because I looked back and gave
23      Austin the all clear. Because that's what it was, all clear!
24      Right, Austin?

25    **AUSTIN:** That's right. Clear as a bird. So slowly and carefully
26      I began to back up and that's when you rear-ended me!

27    **CARLOS:** Yeah. You plowed into my buddy's car.

28    **ALICIA:** No, he plowed into me.

29    **JESSICA:** That's right. Because we both looked back and we

1       **both saw that it was clear.**
2   **AUSTIN: No, because I looked back and saw that it was clear**
3       **before I backed up.**
4   **CARLOS: And I was looking, too. Gave my buddy here the all**
5       **clear. I said, "You're good, man. Back her on up."**
6   **JESSICA: And I was helping Alicia look. I said, "You can go**
7       **now. Nothing's coming."**
8   **AUSTIN: Well, obviously someone here is wrong.**
9   **ALICIA: Which would be you.** *(ALL speak the following at the*
10      *same time as they argue.)*
11  **AUSTIN: You hit me.**
12  **ALICIA: No, you hit me.**
13  **JESSICA: You hit her.**
14  **AUSTIN: It wasn't me.**
15  **CARLOS: No, it was you.**
16  **ALICIA: I was clear to go.**
17  **AUSTIN: No, I was clear to go.**
18  **ALICIA: No, you backed into me.**
19  **AUSTIN: No, you backed into me.**
20  **JESSICA: It was his fault.**
21  **CARLOS: No, it was her fault.**
22  **JESSICA: You hit her.**
23  **CARLOS: You hit him.**
24  **ALICIA: You hit me.**
25  **AUSTIN: No, you hit me.**
26  **LUIS:** *(Enters.)* **Excuse me, but I was walking out of the store**
27      **and I saw what happened.**
28  **AUSTIN: Great! We have a witness.**
29  **ALICIA: Thank you. Now will you please explain to this**
30      **person how he slammed into the back of my car?**
31  **CARLOS: You mean how you slammed into Austin's car.**
32  **AUSTIN: That's right. She slammed into me.**
33  **JESSICA: If we can just get this story right. He backed into**
34      **Alicia's car.** *(Looks at LUIS.)* **Right?**
35  **LUIS: Are you ready to listen to what I saw?** *(ALL nod and say,*

1     *"Yes."*) You both backed out at the exact same time.
2    JESSICA: Which means?
3    LUIS: Which means you both backed out at the exact same
4       time.
5    CARLOS: Which means?
6    LUIS: Which means they are both equally at fault.
7    ALICIA: What?
8    AUSTIN: No way.
9    JESSICA: I don't believe that. Maybe we should call the
10      police.
11   CARLOS: I think that's a good idea.
12   LUIS: Well, if you do, I'll have to stick around since I am a
13      witness.
14   AUSTIN: That's fine with me.
15   ALICIA: Fine with me, too.
16   LUIS: But then I'll have to tell the officer what else I saw.
17   JESSICA: What else did you see?
18   LUIS: *(Points to ALICIA.)* That I saw you texting on your
19      phone as you were backing out.
20   CARLOS: There you go. Guilty party right here.
21   LUIS: *(Points to AUSTIN.)* And I saw you eating a
22      cheeseburger as you backed out.
23   JESSICA: *(To AUSTIN)* See! It was your fault.
24   AUSTIN: I wasn't eating a cheeseburger.
25   LUIS: Looked like one to me.
26   AUSTIN: It was a hamburger. It didn't have any cheese on it.
27   LUIS: Which means if you call the police, you both could get
28      ticketed for reckless driving.
29   CARLOS: Hello, defensive driving.
30   JESSICA: Yeah, and maybe teen court too for the texting and
31      eating while driving. Nowadays that's a big no-no.
32   CARLOS: Get ready to shell out the moolah. All that stuff is
33      expensive.
34   JESSICA: And listen to your parents scream at you. That'd be
35      the worst.

1  ALICIA: I don't want to go to teen court.

2  AUSTIN: And I'm broke. I can't afford all those fines.

3  LUIS: Then I suggest you reevaluate the situation. Come to

4    some sort of agreement.

5  CARLOS: Maybe we can start by surveying the damage.

6  JESSICA: We'll go do the same. *(ALL but LUIS exit. LUIS*

7    *stands alone humming the "Jeopardy" song. After a*

8    *moment, the others enter.)*

9  ALICIA: *(Smiling)* You know what? It was just a little scratch.

10 AUSTIN: Same here. I might even be able to even buff it off.

11 JESSICA: Just an itty-bitty fender bender.

12 CARLOS: I didn't see any major damage.

13 AUSTIN: I say we just shake on it and forget it ever

14    happened. *(Offers his hand.)*

15 ALICIA: *(Shakes hands with him.)* Absolutely! No need to call

16    the police.

17 JESSICA: Over a little ding?

18 CARLOS: That's what they make touch-up paint for.

19 ALICIA: So we'll just be on our way.

20 AUSTIN: Forget it ever happened.

21 CARLOS: I didn't see anything.

22 JESSICA: Me either.

23 LUIS: I did. I saw the whole the thing. Texting, giggling,

24    eating, eating a cheeseburger while searching for

25    French fries ...

26 CARLOS: Hey, you stay out of this.

27 JESSICA: Yeah, it's none of your business.

28 AUSTIN: Yeah! We don't need someone coming along and

29    causing us unnecessary problems.

30 ALICIA: Because we worked it all out, no thanks to you.

31 LUIS: But I'm the one who suggested you reevaluate the

32    situation and work things out. Oh, never mind!

33 ALICIA: *(To JESSICA)* Come on, let's go. *(ALICIA and JESSICA*

34    *exit.)*

35 AUSTIN: *(To CARLOS)* Let's go. *(AUSTIN and CARLOS exit.*

1     *LUIS looks through his bag of purchases for a moment,*
2     *then when he looks up, he is watching ALICIA and*
3     *AUSTIN back out of their parking places again.)*
4  **LUIS: Oh no, here we go again! Someone needs to look back**
5     **while they're backing out of their parking place! Why**
6     **are you girls looking at a magazine? OK, boys, it's up to**
7     **you. You better look back and I mean fast! Great. Go**
8     **ahead and answer that phone. Oh no! It's about to**
9     **happen again. Stop. Stop!** ***Stop!*** *(Covers eyes with hand.*
10    *A loud noise. He puts his hand down and shakes his*
11    *head.)* **And history has repeated itself. So much for a**
12    **little scratch this time. Wow. That's definitely going to**
13    **be some damage worth crying over. And I didn't see a**
14    **thing!** *(As he exits)* **Nope. Didn't see a thing!** *(AUSTIN*
15    *and ALICIA rush to each other, screaming.)*
16  **ALICIA: You hit me!**
17  **AUSTIN: No, you hit me!**
18  **JESSICA:** *(Enters.)* **Did you see what you did? You just backed**
19    **into her car!**
20  **CARLOS:** *(Enters.)* **You did it again! Backed right into his car!**
21  **ALICIA: No, he hit me!**
22  **AUSTIN: No, you hit me!**

# 19. Cheater

CAST: (2F) MORGAN, SOPHIA
SETTING: Sophia's front porch

1  MORGAN: You're avoiding my questions.
2  SOPHIA: No, I'm not. I just don't have to answer your
3      questions.
4  MORGAN: And why not?
5  SOPHIA: Because you're the disgruntled ex-girlfriend who
6      can't stand it that Charlie Ray has moved on. So why
7      don't you take your jealousy and ridiculous stories off
8      my front porch. Go on! Skedaddle!
9  MORGAN: Nice try. Trying to play the innocent act with me.
10     But I know that you knew that Charlie Ray was in a
11     relationship with me when you forced him to cheat.
12 SOPHIA: Forced him?
13 MORGAN: Persuaded him. Confused him. That's what you
14     did! You confused his mind with all your sweet talk and
15     over-exaggerated moves. *(Demonstrates.)* Hey, Charlie
16     Ray, whatcha doin'? Can you help me for a sec? I think
17     the tire on my car looks low. Don't you? Could you just
18     like kinda look at it for me, Charlie Ray?
19 SOPHIA: I didn't do that.
20 MORGAN: Yes you did. You came onto my Charlie Ray.
21 SOHPIA: Charlie Ray and I have been together for six
22     months.
23 MORGAN: *(Shocked)* This has been going on for six months?
24 SOPHIA: Yes, and you need to face the fact that your ex-
25     boyfriend has moved on. I'm Sophia, by the way. And
26     you are ... ?
27 MORGAN: Morgan.
28 SOPHIA: Morgan, I know it can be hard to realize that your
29     ex-boyfriend has fallen in love with someone else, but
       you have got to let it go. I'm sure it was good while it

1  lasted, but you need to face the truth. You and Charlie
2  Ray didn't work out.
3  MORGAN: You don't know what you're talking about.
4  SOPHIA: And there's plenty of other fish in the sea.
5  MORGAN: I realize that you don't realize this, but Charlie
6  Ray and I have been together for a year. Which means,
7  half the time we were together he was cheating on me,
8  but all the time he was seeing you he was cheating on
9  you! You understand? He never broke up with me. We
10  are together. To this day we are together. You and I have
11  both been lied to by Charlie Ray.
12  SOPHIA: That's not true. I don't believe you.
13  MORGAN: OK. So tell me, where were you last night?
14  SOPHIA: Where was I last night? Well, I was at home.
15  MORGAN: Not with Charlie Ray?
16  SOPHIA: No, because he had to work late.
17  MORGAN: Charlie Ray and I were at the racetrack till
18  midnight. His friend Dylan was racing.
19  SOPHIA: You know Dylan?
20  MORGAN: He's Charlie Ray's best friend.
21  SOPHIA: But he said he had to work late stocking inventory.
22  MORGAN: No, he has to do that tonight.
23  SOPHIA: But he's supposed to be with me tonight.
24  MORGAN: Don't fret. He will be.
25  SOPHIA: So you're saying ... he's lying to both of us?
26  MORGAN: I'm sorry, Sophia. I was hurt to find out the truth,
27  too.
28  SOPHIA: Oh, I hate him.
29  MORGAN: Well, I hate him more.
30  SOPHIA: How could you hate him more?
31  MORGAN: Because I had him first and he cheated on me.
32  SOPHIA: With me!
33  MORGAN: I know!
34  SOPHIA: But I hate him more for not telling me that he had
35  a girlfriend when he started pursuing me. So, how did

1     you find out he was lying?

2     MORGAN: Well, last week I saw a movie stub on his desk.

3     *The Bloody Tide.*

4     SOPHIA: Oh my gosh! I saw that. That was such a scary

5     movie. All those people swimming and sunbathing at

6     the beach when out of the blue, hundreds of sharks

7     appear. And they start eating all those people. A leg

8     here, an arm there ...

9     MORGAN: I know. I saw it.

10    SOPHIA: Remember that part when the fat man was

11    struggling to get out of the water and he was so close to

12    reaching the shore and it was all in slow motion.

13    *(Demonstrates.)* The water's up to his waist, he looks

14    back, he sees the sharks coming, and he's trying to

15    reach the shore, when all of a sudden ...

16    MORGAN: That was so disgusting.

17    SOPHIA: But the sharks were too fast. And all of a sudden,

18    he begins screaming as he's pulled into the water. The

19    water is already red from all the other victims, but it

20    becomes even more so. And he's screaming, his arms

21    are reaching up as if asking for help ... and then he goes

22    under. And it's over. That was sad, wasn't it?

23    MORGAN: What was sad is that I had to sit in the movie

24    theatre with Charlie Ray wondering why he hadn't told

25    me he'd already seen the movie before. The week

26    before he'd come over saying he couldn't wait to see

27    this new movie called *The Bloody Tide* and he wanted

28    us to go together. But I knew for a fact he'd already seen

29    it.

30    SOPHIA: With me.

31    MORGAN: Well, at that time I didn't know who he'd seen the

32    movie with. And do you know what he did during the

33    movie?

34    SOPHIA: What?

35    MORGAN: OK, remember the part where the pretty blonde

1      teen was walking along the shore looking for seashells?

2  SOPHIA: Oh my gosh, yes.

3  MORGAN: Of course I didn't know what was about to

4      happen because I'd never seen the movie before. But

5      Charlie Ray leaned over and said, "Watch this!" I mean,

6      how would he know what was going to happen if he

7      hadn't seen the movie before? And I'm halfway

8      watching the movie thinking about all of this when all

9      of a sudden —

10  SOPHIA: Seashells go flying in the air! Chomp! Chomp!

11      Chomp! The monster shark leaps out of the ocean with

12      his jaws wide open and devours her. Chomp! Chomp!

13      Chomp! Then her head was floating in the ocean. That

14      was mega disgusting.

15  MORGAN: And that's when I knew.

16  SOPHIA: When her head was bobbing up and down in the

17      ocean?

18  MORGAN: No! When Charlie Ray said, "Watch this!"

19  SOPHIA: Oh! That's when you knew he was cheating on you?

20  MORGAN: Yes. So for the past week, when we weren't

21      together, I followed him. And that's when I found him

22      with you. Having dinner. At the library. Bowling ...

23  SOPHIA: You followed us? Then why didn't you come over

24      and say something?

25  MORGAN: And say what? "Excuse me, that's my boyfriend

26      you're with?" And fight over him?

27  SOPHIA: Do you think we should?

28  MORGAN: What?

29  SOPHIA: Fight over Charlie Ray?

30  MORGAN: No. You can have him.

31  SOPHIA: But if he's cheating on me, I don't want him.

32  MORGAN: Well, I sure don't want him. Don't worry about it.

33      He's yours.

34  SOPHIA: No, you can have him back. I'm stepping away. I

35      apologize for not knowing that he was taken. He's all

1    yours now.

2    MORGAN: No thank you. I don't want a boyfriend who
3       cheats. He's all yours.

4    SOPHIA: No, he was yours first. You take him.

5    MORGAN: But I don't want him.

6    SOPHIA: Neither do I.

7    MORGAN: I insist. He's yours.

8    SOPHIA: Well, I insist that you take him.

9    MORGAN: No, you take him.

10   SOPHIA: No, you.

11   MORGAN: You.

12   SOPHIA: You.

13   MORGAN: You!

14   SOPHIA: You!

15   MORGAN: Then maybe neither one of us wants him.

16   SOPHIA: That's fine with me.

17   MORGAN: Me too. *(Pause)*

18   SOPHIA: So, are you going to break up with him?

19   MORGAN: I am. I'm going to invite him over then tell him I
20      never want to see his face again.

21   SOPHIA: Or better yet, why don't we both show up at his
22      work this afternoon, together, and confront him.

23   MORGAN: Good idea. "Charlie Ray, you've been caught!"

24   SOPHIA: "You're a cheater, Charlie Ray!" Maybe we should
25      announce it on the store's intercom just to make sure
26      he hears us loud and clear.

27   MORGAN: That would be nice. "Attention everyone! Charlie
28      Ray is a cheater!"

29   SOPHIA: Yes! And I'll add, "And a lying piece of scum!"

30   MORGAN: I like that. "Lying piece of scum! And how dare
31      you sneak around our backs and cheat on us ... "

32   SOPHIA and MORGAN: "You lying piece of scum!"

33   SOPHIA: "The games are over, Charlie Ray."

34   MORGAN: "Because we are finished. Both of us."

35   SOPHIA and MORGAN: "You lying piece of scum!"

1   MORGAN: "And I'm glad I found out what you did, because
2       unlike you, I can hold my head up high, but you ... "
3   SOPHIA: "You disgust me and you're nothing but ... "
4   SOPHIA and MORGAN: "A lying piece of scum!"
5   MORGAN: "And if I could make one wish, I'd wish that you
6       were surfing in the ocean ... "
7   SOPHIA: "And *The Bloody Tide* was based on a true story."
8   MORGAN: "Yeah! And as you were showing off your pathetic
9       muscles to your newest girlfriend ... "
10  SOPHIA: "Standing knee deep in the ocean ... "
11  MORGAN: "The sharks move in closer ... "
12  SOPHIA: "And closer ... "
13  MORGAN: "Until ... "
14  SOPHIA and MORGAN: "Chomp! Chomp! Chomp!"
15  SOPHIA: "And don't think I'd cry one single tear."
16  MORGAN: "No, not one."
17  SOPHIA: "But what would I say?"
18  MORGAN: *(Shrugs.)* "Oh well."
19  SOPHIA: *(Shrugs.)* "Too bad."
20  MORGAN: "Because you know what you are, Charlie Ray?"
21  SOPHIA and MORGAN: "You're a lying piece of scum!"
22  SOPHIA: Yeah, that's what we'd say.
23  MORGAN: And that's what we're going to say. Come on.
24  SOPHIA: Where are we going?
25  MORGAN: Where do you think?
26  SOPHIA: *(Smiles.)* To Charlie Ray's work.
27  MORGAN: I'll race you to the store microphone.
28  SOPHIA: You're on! *(They rush off.)*

# 20. Accidents Happen

CAST: (5M, 1F) NICOLE, SEAN, CALEB, JACK, RAY, BUBBA
PROPS: Boy's shirt, baseball cap
SETTING: An alley

1    *(At rise, NICOLE is wearing a boy's shirt and has her hair*
2    *tucked inside a baseball cap.)*
3    **NICOLE: Why am I doing this?**
4    **SEAN:** *(Looking around)* **I need some backup.**
5    **NICOLE: And you couldn't find a guy to back you up?**
6    **SEAN: Phil and Sid are at basketball practice. I needed**
7    **someone fast. Like now!**
8    **NICOLE: Do I look like a boy?**
9    **SEAN: I guess.**
10   **NICOLE: I do?**
11   **SEAN: But you don't talk like one.**
12   **NICOLE:** *(Lowers her voice.)* **OK, how does this sound? Do I**
13   **sound like a boy now?**
14   **SEAN: Sure.**
15   **NICOLE: So what am I supposed to do?**
16   **SEAN: Stand there and look mean.**
17   **NICOLE: OK.** *(Glares.)* **Is this good?**
18   **SEAN: Yeah, I guess. And maybe at some point you could do**
19   **this.** *(Slams fist into hand.)* **Like you're ready to fight.**
20   **NICOLE:** *(Slams fist into hand.)* **Bring it on, boys!**
21   **SEAN:** *(Looks at watch.)* **They said four o'clock sharp behind**
22   **Mickey's Hardware Store. Wonder where they are?**
23   **NICOLE: Maybe they didn't really mean it.**
24   **SEAN: Oh, they meant it all right. Believe me, they meant it.**
25   **NICOLE: How many are coming?**
26   **SEAN: Just Caleb and his sidekick. Two.**
27   **NICOLE: Two on two. That's OK. We can take them down.**
28   **SEAN: You're not fighting them, Nicole.**
29   **NICOLE: I can do my part here.**

1 SEAN: No. You're just here to give me some support. Maybe
2     when Caleb sees it's two of us, he'll back down.
3 NICOLE: Well, I'm not backing down. I'm ready to take
4     these guys on. *(Hits fist into her hand then shakes it out.)*
5     Ouch.
6 SEAN: Maybe we'll be able to talk it out.
7 NICOLE: You want me to do the talking?
8 SEAN: No, because you sound like a girl.
9 NICOLE: Because I am a girl, Sean! But I'm going to lower
10     my voice like this. *(Lowers voice.)* Hey, let's talk about
11     this first.
12 SEAN: No, you let me do the talking. All you have to do is
13     stand there and look mean.
14 NICOLE: I can do that. *(Glares, then hits fist into hand. Again,*
15     *she shakes it out. CALEB, JACK, RAY, and BUBBA enter.)*
16 CALEB: I thought you'd chicken out.
17 SEAN: Why would I?
18 NICOLE: *(Leans over to speak to SEAN.)* Uh, do you want to
19     run for it? I think we're outnumbered here.
20 CALEB: What'd you say?
21 NICOLE: Who, me? *(Lowers voice.)* I mean, who, me?
22 CALEB: What's wrong with your voice?
23 NICOLE: Sore throat. *(Slams fist into hand.)* So what's the
24     problem, dudes?
25 CALEB: You know what my problem is, Sean. Don't you?
26 SEAN: Yeah, well, I ... Yeah.
27 CALEB: Let me introduce you to my friends. Jack.
28 JACK: Hey.
29 CALEB: Ray.
30 RAY: You're going down, man.
31 CALEB: And Bubba. Bubba doesn't talk much. Do ya,
32     Bubba? *(BUBBA grunts.)*
33 JACK: Let's get this over with.
34 RAY: Won't take two seconds. *(BUBBA grunts, then hits fist*
35     *into hand. NICOLE then grunts and hits her fist into her*
36     *hand.)*

1 NICOLE: Bring it on!

2 SEAN: You don't want to talk first?

3 CALEB: What's there to talk about? You have to pay for what

4     you did.

5 SEAN: Caleb, I told you it was an accident. Why can't you

6     believe me?

7 NICOLE: Yeah, why can't you believe him?

8 JACK: Let me at him, Caleb. I'm ready to take him down.

9 RAY: And I'll take the other one. And Bubba, you can finish

10     the job. Just to make sure they stay down for a long

11     time. *(BUBBA grunts. Slams his fist into his hand.*

12     *NICOLE also slams her fist into her hand and grunts.)*

13 CALEB: Oh, you wanna talk, Sean? Sit down and have a little

14     powwow?

15 SEAN: I just wanted to explain —

16 RAY: This ought to be funny, Caleb. Let him explain.

17 JACK: Yeah, and after he explains, we'll explain it to him in

18     our own way. *(BUBBA grunts and slams fist into hand.*

19     *NICOLE does the same.)*

20 CALEB: Sure, Sean. Go ahead. You have one minute.

21 NICOLE: I'd like to hear this too, Sean.

22 CALEB: You don't know?

23 NICOLE: No, he didn't tell me. I'm just here for backup. *(Hits*

24     *fist into hand.)* So go ahead, Sean. Tell him why you did

25     whatever it is you did.

26 SEAN: I told you it was an accident.

27 CALEB: Why don't you let me explain it to your friend here?

28     What's your name?

29 NICOLE: Uh —

30 SEAN: *(Quickly)* Stone.

31 NICOLE: Yeah! Stone.

32 CALEB: Well, let me tell you, Stone, what your buddy did at

33     school.

34 NICOLE: I'm listening.

35 CALEB: Picture the lunchroom. Crowded. I mean packed.

1  My boys are sitting at the table waiting on me. Right,
2  boys?
3  JACK, RAY, and BUBBA: Yeah. That's right.
4  CALEB: So I'm walking across the middle of the lunchroom
5      and Sean thinks it would be funny to stick his leg out
6      and trip me.
7  SEAN: I told you it was an accident!
8  NICOLE: You tripped him?
9  SEAN: It was an accident!
10 CALEB: And you expect me to believe that? So there I went.
11     My tray and all my food went flying across the room.
12     And I fell flat on my face in front of the entire
13     lunchroom. You should have seen everyone in there.
14     Laughing. Pointing.
15 JACK: But we weren't laughing.
16 RAY: No. We were steaming mad and if we hadn't been at
17     school ... *(Shakes his head. BUBBA grunts and slams his*
18     *fist into his hand.)*
19 NICOLE: Hold on here a minute. Just hold on. I want a few
20     more details to this story.
21 JACK: What's the point?
22 RAY: You just heard what happened. And now it's time to
23     pay. Right, Caleb?
24 CALEB: Right.
25 NICOLE: Just a minute. Hold your horses. I have a few
26     questions I'd like answered first.
27 CALEB: What?
28 NICOLE: Sean, did you purposely trip Caleb?
29 SEAN: No! I've said all along it was an accident.
30 NICOLE: Then how do you explain what happened?
31 SEAN: Well, I had just finished eating and I leaned back to
32     stretch out my legs. That's when Caleb walked by and
33     tripped.
34 CALEB: No, you did it on purpose.
35 RAY: Let's get this over with, Caleb.

1   JACK: We're ready. Just give us the word.

2   CALEB: Do it!

3   NICOLE: Hold on! Hold on!

4   CALEB: Why?

5   NICOLE: Because!

6   CALEB: Because?

7   NICOLE: Because I want to ask you something first.

8   CALEB: What?

9   NICOLE: Have you never done anything on accident in your

10      life? Ever?

11  CALEB: No. Have you?

12  NICOLE: Well, sure. One time I was playing Barbies with my

13      sister —

14  CALEB: Playing Barbies?

15  NICOLE: I mean, playing with these green army men! It was

16      my sister who was playing with the Barbies.

17  CALEB: So what happened?

18  NICOLE: I was getting into the whole war scene, you know.

19      Had the army men lined up across the mound of dirt,

20      ready to fight the uh ... Barbies.

21  CALEB: The army men were going to fight the Barbies?

22  NICOLE: Yeah! We were outnumbered, too. Just like today.

23      And anyway, one of my army men decided to torpedo

24      one of the Barbies so I slung a rock in that direction.

25      But the rock didn't hit the Barbie; it hit my seven-year-

26      old sister.

27  JACK: Oh no! Was she OK?

28  RAY: I hope you didn't put out her eye.

29  NICOLE: I put a nice sized gash in her forehead. She had to

30      get stitches. I felt like the worst person ever.

31  CALEB: Yeah, well, you didn't do it on purpose.

32  NICOLE: Yeah, well neither did Sean.

33  CALEB: I don't believe that.

34  JACK: Neither do I.

35  RAY: I don't either. *(BUBBA grunts.)*

1   NICOLE: So you're telling me you've never done anything on
2        accident before? Ever?
3   RAY: I did. Last summer I didn't lock the back gate and my
4        dog got out and ... *(Starts to cry)* Precious got hit by a car!
5   NICOLE: And I bet you didn't do it on purpose, did you?
6   RAY: No! I loved that dog.
7   JACK: I did something on accident, too.
8   CALEB: *(Throws his hands in the air.)* I don't believe this.
9   NICOLE: What did you do, Jack?
10  JACK: Fell off my bike and dropped my school pictures in
11       the mud. My mom was so mad. But I kept telling her it
12       was an accident. And it was! But she thought I did it on
13       purpose because I didn't like my pictures.
14  NICOLE: I'm sorry that happened.
15  JACK: Thanks.
16  NICOLE: Bubba, anything like that ever happen to you?
17  BUBBA: *(Growls. A pause)* Yeah.
18  NICOLE: What, Bubba?
19  BUBBA: I broke my mom's favorite crystal bowl.
20  JACK: What happened?
21  CALEB: Who cares what happened! Let's take care of Sean.
22       *(Hits fist into hand.)* Come on, guys. Come on, Bubba!
23       That's what we came here to do. That's why we're
24       standing in the alley behind Mickey's Hardware Store.
25  BUBBA: I was carrying my mom's crystal bowl to the table
26       on Thanksgiving Day and my little niece came up and
27       started tickling me. And I was like ... *(Laughs in a girly*
28       *way, then demonstrates dropping the bowl)* and I was
29       laughing and I dropped the bowl and it fell. Mashed
30       potatoes all over the floor. Mom's crystal bowl,
31       shattered.
32  NICOLE: And it was an accident, right?
33  BUBBA: Of course.
34  NICOLE: Of course it was.
35  CALEB: OK, now that we've all shared a touching little story
36       here.

1 NICOLE: What about you, Caleb?

2 CALEB: What about me?

3 NICOLE: You haven't ever done anything on accident before

4     in your life?

5 CALEB: No!

6 JACK: Come on, Caleb.

7 RAY: Sure you have.

8 BUBBA: You did last week.

9 CALEB: What are you talking about, Bubba?

10 BUBBA: After the movie was over and we came out of that

11     dark theatre you accidentally walked into the women's

12     restroom.

13 CALEB: Shut up, Bubba!

14 BUBBA: Hey, you didn't mean to.

15 CALEB: No, of course I didn't mean to.

16 BUBBA: And all those women were screaming. "Get out! Get

17     out! Get out you pervert!" And you came running out

18     like a mad man.

19 NICOLE: See! You're not perfect either, Caleb. Everyone

20     messes up from time to time. Accidents happen.

21 SEAN: So can we just forget about this, Caleb?

22 CALEB: I don't think so.

23 RAY: Maybe you should, Caleb.

24 JACK: I agree.

25 BUBBA: Let it go, man.

26 CALEB: No! I came here to fight and that's what I'm going to

27     do.

28 NICOLE: *(Steps up.)* Then why don't you fight me if you want

29     to fight someone?

30 CALEB: OK! Let's go.

31 SEAN: *(To NICOLE)* No, don't do it.

32 NICOLE: Stay out of this, Sean.

33 CALEB: You want me and you to handle this? Well, I'm fine

34     about it. You've been all in up our business anyway, so

35     you can just take the fall for it.

1   **NICOLE: Fine with me, too.**

2   **CALEB: So show me what you've got, Stone.**

3   **RAY: Come on, Caleb. Let it go.**

4   **JACK: Let's just leave.**

5   **BUBBA: I don't want to see you two fight.**

6   **SEAN: Me neither. I really don't want to see you two fight.**

7   **NICOLE:** *(Putting up her fists)* **Stay out of it, Sean.**

8   **CALEB:** *(Puts up his fist.)* **Come on, show me what you've got.**

9       **Come on. Go ahead! Hit me. Come on. Hit me!** *(NICOLE*

10      *punches him in the stomach and he falls to the ground*

11      *crying. SEAN pulls off NICOLE's hat, her hair falls down,*

12      *and all the BOYS see that she is a girl.)*

13   **CALEB:** *(Looks up.)* **You're a girl?**

14   **NICOLE: Now why don't you apologize to Sean for not**

15      **believing that he tripped you on accident?**

16   **CALEB:** *(Shakes his head until NICOLE hits her fist into her*

17      *hand.)* **I'm sorry!**

18   **SEAN: I'm sorry too. I really didn't mean to trip you.** *(Helps*

19      *CALEB stand.)*

20   **CALEB: I know. I should've let it go. Hey, maybe tomorrow**

21      **you can come sit with me and the guys at lunch.**

22   **SEAN: Sure. I'd like that.**

23   **CALEB: And bring your backup girl with you if you want.**

24      **Man, she's one tough girl. Does she have a boyfriend?**

25   **SEAN: I'm pretty sure she's available.**

26   **CALEB: Good, good.** *(SEAN and CALEB exit.)*

27   **RAY: That was some right-handed punch you threw there.**

28   **JACK: I was impressed.**

29   **BUBBA: Especially for a girl.** *(He smiles, hits fist into hand.)*

30   **NICOLE:** *(She smiles back, hits fist into hand.)* **Come on. Let's**

31      **go get some ice cream or something. I'm hungry.**

32   **RAY: Me too.**

33   **JACK: I'm in.**

34   **BUBBA: Bubble gum ice cream for me.**

35   **NICOLE: That's my favorite, too, Bubba!** *(They exit,*

36      *laughing.)*

# 21. The Birds and the Bees

CAST: (4F) PAIGE, KELLY, TARA, AMBER
SETTING: Auditorium

1     *(At rise, the GIRLS are sitting in an auditorium staring*
2     *straight ahead with blank expressions on their faces.*
3     *Suddenly, AMBER laughs out loud, then quickly covers*
4     *her mouth with her hand.)*
5   **PAIGE: Amber, it's not funny.**
6   **KELLY: Yeah, it's embarrassing.**
7   **TARA: At least there are no boys in here.**
8   **PAIGE: The boys have their own assembly next week.**
9   **AMBER: I'm sorry, but I thought it was funny.**
10  **PAIGE: Shhhh ... Be quiet before we get into trouble.** *(The*
11     *GIRLS stare straight ahead. After a moment, AMBER*
12     *laughs out loud again. The OTHER GIRLS look at her.)*
13  **AMBER: I'm sorry! I can't help it.**
14  **TARA: Amber, what are you laughing at?**
15  **AMBER: The pictures that Mrs. Wilson is drawing.** *(The*
16     *GIRLS tilt their heads sideways to the right)*
17  **KELLY: That doesn't look right.**
18  **TARA: It's confusing.**
19  **KELLY: I don't get it.**
20  **AMBER: No, it's funny. Look at the smiley face that Mrs.**
21     **Wilson gave that little ... that little ... what is that? A**
22     **fish?**
23  **TARA: It's a fish?**
24  **KELLY: It's not a fish.**
25  **PAIGE: It's a baby.**
26  **TARA: Not yet. But it will be.** *(The GIRLS tilt their heads to the*
27     *left as they give a confused look.)*
28  **PAIGE: That's weird.**

1   **AMBER: Is that a baby without arms and legs?**

2   **KELLY: I think so.**

3   **PAIGE: I can't believe she just said that.**

4   **TARA: I'm glad there are no boys in here.**

5   **KELLY: At least she's not drawing a picture of it.**

6   **AMBER: Again, you spoke too soon.** *(The GIRLS look ahead as*

7       *they giggle and nudge each other.)*

8   **PAIGE: Good, she's moving onto something else.** *(Pause as*

9       *they listen. After a moment, AMBER bursts out laughing.)*

10  **KELLY: Amber!**

11  **TARA: Shhhh!**

12  **KELLY: Did I miss something?**

13  **AMBER:** *(Snickering)* **Did you hear what Mrs. Wilson said?**

14  **KELLY: What?**

15  **AMBER: About us talking to our parents about sex?**

16  **PAIGE: Uh ... like, no!**

17  **TARA: I'd rather die.**

18  **AMBER: And we should approach our parents about sex**

19     **before they approach us?**

20  **KELLY: Why would I approach my parents? I already know**

21     **everything.**

22  **TARA: What's she drawing now?**

23  **PAIGE: I don't get it.**

24  **TARA: Is that what we used to look like?**

25  **PAIGE: A big blob of cells?**

26  **KELLY: I never looked like that.**

27  **AMBER: Me neither.**

28  **KELLY: What did Mrs. Wilson say?**

29  **TARA: Human reproduction is the reproduction of**

30     **humans?**

31  **PAIGE: It's what?**

32  **KELLY: Human reproduction is the reproduction of**

33     **humans.**

34  **AMBER: That's deep.**

35  **TARA: And we actually have to learn this stuff?**

1   **AMBER: Question: Why do some people call it "the birds**
2        **and the bees"? Don't birds lay eggs?**
3   **TARA: Yeah! We don't lay eggs.**
4   **KELLY: Come on, guys. We need to listen.**
5   **TARA: I'm still confused.**
6   **PAIGE: Then maybe we should pay attention.** *(The GIRLS*
7        *nod and stare straight ahead.)*
8   **AMBER: How do bees have babies?**
9   **KELLY: I don't have a clue.**
10  **PAIGE: What is Mrs. Wilson doing now?**
11  **TARA: What's with the sound effects?** *(Makes a strange*
12       *noise.)*
13  **KELLY: I guess that's the sound of human reproduction.**
14  **PAIGE: That's weird.**
15  **KELLY: And now she's singing? Really?**
16  **AMBER: What is she singing?**
17  **PAIGE: Babies come from a mommy and a daddy?**
18  **TARA: Babies come from a mommy and daddy? Duh!** *(The*
19      *GIRLS stare straight ahead.)*
20  **TARA: What is she drawing now?**
21  **PAIGE: I think it's supposed to be the birth of a baby.**
22  **KELLY: Ewwww! I'm not having kids!**
23  **PAIGE: Me neither!**
24  **AMBER: I'm having puppies.** *(The GIRLS all look at her.)* **Not**
25       **having puppies like having puppies, but have a dog**
26       **that has puppies.**
27  **PAIGE: Are we supposed to be taking notes?**
28  **AMBER: I hope not.**
29  **KELLY: What's that? XX chromosomes are girls?**
30  **TARA: And XY chromosomes are boys?**
31  **AMBER: What's an XYZ?** *(Raises hand.)* **I'll ask.** *(The OTHER*
32      *GIRLS pull her hand down.)*
33  **PAIGE: There is no XYZ.**
34  **KELLY: That's stupid.**
35  **AMBER: Hey, I didn't know.**

1   KELLY: Great! Mrs. Wilson is singing another song.
2      "Abstinence is the best policy."
3   PAIGE: I believe in abstinence.
4   AMBER: Me too.
5   TARA: Me three.
6   KELLY: Me four. *(Points.)* Because I don't want to have one of
7      those.
8   AMBER: I'm sticking with puppies.
9   KELLY: Look!
10  PAIGE: Oh my gosh!
11  TARA: What is Mrs. Wilson doing now?
12  PAIGE: And why is she screaming?
13  TARA: Is she OK?
14  AMBER: Is Mrs. Wilson having a baby on the stage?
15  KELLY: I think it's a demonstration.
16  TARA: Is she trying to scare us?
17  KELLY: She's scaring me.
18  TARA: Me too.
19  PAIGE: Why would the teachers let her do this?
20  AMBER: I wish she would stop screaming.
21  KELLY: I think she is trying to scare us.
22  PAIGE: Yeah, scare us from having a baby.
23  TARA: I'm scared.
24  KELLY: Me too.
25  AMBER: You know, after this, I'm definitely having puppies.

# 22. Carnival Games

CAST: (2M, 2F) ALEXIS, JOSIE, ERIC, CARTER
PROPS: Stuffed animals, pencil, plastic toy, balloon
SETTING: Carnival

1     *(At rise, ALEXIS and JOSIE are watching their boyfriends*
2     *play games at the carnival. ALEXIS holds several large*
3     *stuffed animals while JOSIE holds a few small items such*
4     *as a pencil, plastic toy, etc.)*
5  **ALEXIS:** *(Yelling)* **Carter, you can do it! And I want the pink**
6     **teddy bear with the heart-shaped nose.** *(Another stuffed*
7     *animal can be described to match prop.)*
8  **JOSIE: The ring toss is hard. I think Eric has already spent**
9     **ten dollars trying to get one of those rings around the**
10    **glass bottles.**
11  **ALEXIS: Carter can do it.** *(Looks at JOSIE.)* **What has Eric won**
12    **for you?**
13  **JOSIE: Oh, a pencil, plastic toy, and a broken compass. I**
14    **think the games at the carnival are pretty much rigged.**
15  **ALEXIS:** *(Ignoring her comment and holding up a stuffed*
16    *animal)* **Don't you just love this one? Isn't he cute?** *(Hugs*
17    *the animal.)*
18  **JOSIE: How do you know it's a he?**
19  **ALEXIS:** *(Kisses the animal.)* **Because I named him Carter,**
20    **after my boyfriend.**
21  **ERIC:** *(Enters.)* **That ring toss is rigged! I tried everything,**
22    **but every time it bounced right off. Oh, I got a**
23    **consolation prize for you. I guess the carny lady felt**
24    **sorry for me and handed me this balloon. Do you want**
25    **me to blow it up for you?**
26  **JOSIE: No, that's OK. Thanks.**
27  **ERIC: Yeah, ten bucks for a stupid balloon. That game is**
28    **rigged to the max.** *(Yells.)* **Your game is rigged, people!**
29  **ALEXIS:** *(Jumps up and down.)* **Carter did it. He just landed**

1   **that red ring on the glass bottle. You won! You won!**

2 **ERIC: Lucky.**

3 **CARTER:** *(Enters with a large stuffed animal.)* **Look what I got**

4   **for you.**

5 **ALEXIS: I love it!** *(Shows the others.)* **Isn't he cute? Oh, he's so**

6   **cute.**

7 **CARTER: What did you get, Josie?**

8 **JOSIE: A balloon.**

9 **CARTER: That's all?**

10 **JOSIE: And a pencil, a plastic toy, and a compass.**

11 **ALEXIS: Her compass is broken.**

12 **ERIC: Your compass is broken?**

13 **JOSIE: It's OK.**

14 **ERIC: That's wrong. I spent twenty bucks for a plastic**

15   **compass that doesn't even work.**

16 **JOSIE: Really, it's OK, Eric.**

17 **ALEXIS: What should we do next?**

18 **CARTER:** *(Pointing)* **I want to try that one.**

19 **ERIC: The basketball game?**

20 **CARTER: That looks easy. I can do that.**

21 **ERIC: Sure, sure. Step right up. Step right up. Be the**

22   **boyfriend that your girl will love. Simply whisk this**

23   **basketball into the basket and you win.**

24 **ALEXIS: You can do it Carter.**

25 **CARTER:** *(Kisses ALEXIS on the cheek.)* **I'll win you a prize.**

26 **ALEXIS: I like the giraffe. Yes! Win me the giraffe!** *(Or*

27   *another animal he wins.)*

28 **CARTER: No problem.** *(Exits.)*

29 **ALEXIS:** *(Jumps up and down.)* **I love the carnival!**

30 **ERIC: There's no way he can win at that game. I've watched**

31   **at least twenty-five grown men attempt to shoot a ball**

32   **into the basket and they couldn't do it. I'm telling you**

33   **it's rigged.**

34 **ALEXIS: I don't believe you.**

35 **JOSIE: I do.**

1　ERIC: It is rigged. The basketballs are a larger size than
2　　　　normal and the hoops are smaller. I'm telling you, you
3　　　　just can't win at this game! *(Looks ahead.)* See?
4　ALEXIS: *(Yells.)* You can do it, Carter.
5　JOSIE: Carter is wasting his money.
6　ALEXIS: He has one more shot. *(Pause as they watch. Then*
7　　　　*ALEXIS jumps up and down.)* Yes, he did it. He did it!
8　ERIC: I can't believe this. There's no way ...
9　JOSIE: I've heard the games are rigged, too. He was just
10　　　　lucky.
11　CARTER: *(Enters with another stuffed animal.)* Here you go.
12　ALEXIS: *(Throws her arms around CARTER.)* Thank you!
13　　　　Thank you! You are so wonderful.
14　CARTER: Thank you, Alexis.
15　ALEXIS: Carter, would it hurt your feelings if I gave Josie
16　　　　one of my stuffed animals?
17　CARTER: No, not at all.
18　JOSIE: No, it's OK.
19　ALEXIS: *(Holds out a stuffed animal.)* Here.
20　JOSIE: No, it's yours. I couldn't.
21　ALEXIS: Yes, take it. Please.
22　CARTER: It's fine with me.
23　JOSIE: No, really.
24　ERIC: That's it! That is it!
25　ALEXIS: What?
26　JOSIE: What's wrong, Eric?
27　ERIC: *(Turns to JOSIE.)* I'm going to win you a stuffed animal
28　　　　if it breaks me.
29　JOSIE: No, Eric!
30　ERIC: Yes! *(Points.)* Right there. At the Milk Bottle Throw.
31　　　　I'm going to hit those bottles so hard and smash them
32　　　　onto the ground and win you a stuffed animal.
33　ALEXIS: That looks easy.
34　CARTER: You can do it.
35　ERIC: I'm going to. You just watch me.

1 JOSIE: *(As ERIC exits.)* **Good luck.**
2 CARTER: Actually, that game is harder than it looks.
3 ALEXIS: How hard can it be? You just knock over some
4     dumb ol' bottles with a ball.
5 CARTER: *(Shaking his head)* Those bottles are weighed
6     down. There's a trick to it. Actually there's a trick to all
7     these games. You just have to know the secret.
8 JOSIE: Well, go up there and tell Eric how it's done.
9 CARTER: I can't do that.
10 JOSIE: Why not?
11 CARTER: Because I haven't figured that one out yet. I've
12     tried. Knocked a few of the milk bottles over, but
13     there's always one left standing.
14 JOSIE: *(Hollers.)* **Come on, Eric. You can do it.**
15 CARTER: Bet he can't. *(JOSIE looks at him.)* **But I hope he**
16     can.
17 ALEXIS: *(Yells.)* **That's OK. Try it again.**
18 JOSIE: *(Yells.)* **Knock 'em all down, Eric. You can do it.**
19 CARTER: *(Yells.)* **Almost. Bet you get them all down next**
20     time. *(ALL watch with anticipation, then show*
21     *disappointment.)*
22 ERIC: *(Enters, throwing his hands up in the air.)* **Nothing!**
23 JOSIE: It's no big deal, Eric.
24 ALEXIS: You almost knocked them all over.
25 CARTER: I couldn't even do that one.
26 ERIC: Well, I'm not giving up. *(Points.)* **That one.**
27 JOSIE: The Balloon Dart Throw?
28 ERIC: Now that I can do. *(Exits.)*
29 JOSIE: Good luck!
30 ALEXIS: Yeah, good luck!
31 CARTER: That's another one I don't play.
32 ALEXIS: Why not?
33 CARTER: It's rigged. The balloons are underinflated and
34     the dart tips are dull.
35 JOSIE: Why didn't you tell him that?

1    CARTER: And there's another problem. The prizes are
2    usually dinky in this game. You have to keep trading up
3    over and over to win a decent prize. That's why I don't
4    like this game.
5    ALEXIS: *(Looking on)* Come on, Eric.
6    JOSIE: *(Watching ERIC, then jumping up and down)* You did
7    it!
8    ALEXIS: He did it! *(Jumps up and down with JOSIE.)*
9    CARTER: I figured he'd get at least one. But the prizes ...
10    *(Shakes his head.)*
11    ERIC: *(Enters looking disappointed.)* I just spent my last five
12    bucks.
13    JOSIE: But you won!
14    ERIC: *(Holds out a plastic ring.)* For this.
15    JOSIE: *(Takes the ring.)* Oh.
16    ALEXIS: *(Trying to help)* That's cute. I like it.
17    ERIC: Five dollars for a stupid plastic ring.
18    JOSIE: No, I love it! *(Attempts to put it on.)* But it's a little ... a
19    little ... small.
20    ERIC: I'd have to trade up several more times to get you a
21    stuffed animal. The next prize up was a shot glass. For
22    ten dollars I could have gotten you a plastic shot glass.
23    Then for another five dollars I could've gotten you a
24    deluxe hand clapper. Now we're at fifteen dollars. And
25    that's assuming I pop another balloon. Then I could get
26    you a squirt camera on up to a mini SpongeBob pillow.
27    Then I could've traded ol' SpongeBob in for a felt pirate
28    hat. Bet you would love that, huh? Then I could've
29    traded your felt pirate hat in for a crazy loop straw.
30    Then from there an inflatable guitar and then finally,
31    finally, a medium stuffed animal of your choice. I'd
32    have to bust out another ten or so balloons for a large
33    stuffed animal. And for one of those giant ones, well,
34    I'd be there all night. Throwing dull darts and popping
35    underinflated balloons. So you know what?

1  JOSIE: What?

2  ERIC: I hope you like your plastic ring because I'm broke.

3  JOSIE: I love it, Eric. Really I do.

4  ALEXIS: I love it too. I love it so much that'd I'd trade you

5      one of my stuffed animals for it.

6  ERIC: No you wouldn't.

7  ALEXIS: Yes I would.

8  CARTER: It's true. Alexis wanted a ring and I couldn't even

9      win her one. Gosh, I'm sorry, Alexis.

10 ALEXIS: It's OK. Josie, would you trade me your ring for one

11     of my animals?

12 JOSIE: No thank you. I love my ring.

13 CARTER: Hey, look. I've still got two bucks left. Come on,

14     Eric. I'll give you a dollar and we'll each get ten dimes

15     and toss them on the plates for a prize.

16 ERIC: No one ever wins at that.

17 CARTER: Well, let's go try.

18 ERIC: OK. *(The BOYS exit.)*

19 ALEXIS: Carter is right. No one ever wins that one. I think

20     they coat the plates with WD-40.

21 JOSIE: Probably. *(Looking at ALEXIS)* Wow. Look at you.

22 ALEXIS: *(Hugging the stuffed animals)* I know. And I just love

23     them all.

24 JOSIE: *(Looks at her items.)* I bet Eric spent fifty dollars on

25     this stuff.

26 ALEXIS: At least. But we had fun, didn't we?

27 JOSIE: Yes, we did. *(Looking ahead)* I wonder how they're

28     doing tossing dimes on plates? I did that once and they

29     all slid off.

30 ALEXIS: Me too. I suggest that when the boys finish playing

31     games, we should head over to the Ferris wheel.

32 JOSIE: Good idea. I love the Ferris wheel.

33 ALEXIS: Are you sure I can't trade you a stuffed animal for

34     your ring?

35 JOSIE: *(Laughs.)* I'm sure. But if you want my broken

36     compass ...

1   ALEXIS: *(Laughs.)* No!
2   CARTER: *(Enters looking sad.)* I lost.
3   ALEXIS: It's OK.
4   JOSIE: Where's Eric?
5   CARTER: Pulling himself together. He's really upset he
6        couldn't win a stuffed animal.
7   JOSIE: Is he all right?
8   CARTER: I think he needs a minute.
9   ALEXIS: Well, when he gets back we'd like to go over to the
10       Ferris wheel. No more carnival games.
11  JOSIE: I agree. Such a waste of money.
12  ERIC: *(Enters holding a stuffed animal.)* Josie, look what I
13       won for you!
14  JOSIE: What?
15  ALEXIS: You won? Carter, you were teasing us.
16  CARTER: I was! Second coin he tossed stayed on the plate. I
17       couldn't believe it.
18  ERIC: *(Hands JOSIE the stuffed animal.)* For you.
19  JOSIE: I love it! I really love it!
20  ALEXIS: OK guys, we're going to the Ferris wheel now. No
21       more carnival games.
22  ERIC: Sounds like a good plan.

# 23. Screaming Bloody Murder

CAST: (3F) SIERRA, MOLLY, ERIN
PROPS: Three chairs, book
SETTING: Kitchen

1   *(At rise, SIERRA and MOLLY are each standing on a chair,*
2   *looking down at the floor. SIERRA is holding a book.)*
3   **SIERRA: Go away!**
4   **MOLLY: I don't think he heard you.**
5   **SIERRA: Go away! Do you hear me? Go away!**
6   **MOLLY: Either the scorpion is ignoring you or he's happy**
7   **where he's at.**
8   **SIERRA: You know, the only time I saw my mother cry was**
9   **when a scorpion bit her. I had to call Dad at work and**
10  **he rushed home to see her. She said it hurt like you-**
11  **know-what.**
12  **MOLLY: That's why I'm staying up here.**
13  **SIERRA: Which may be all night, Molly. Because my parents**
14  **won't be home from their trip until tomorrow.**
15  **MOLLY: Which means we have to sleep standing up?**
16  **SIERRA: Or stay awake all night. Unless of course** *(Screams)*
17  ***the stupid scorpion decides to crawl back from where it***
18  ***came!***
19  **MOLLY: Too bad it looks so content. Like it's napping on the**
20  **ceramic tile in your kitchen.**
21  **SIERRA:** *Go away!*
22  **MOLLY: We should have stayed in your room to study.**
23  **SIERRA: But we were hungry. I'm still hungry. Too bad the**
24  **pantry is way over there.**
25  **MOLLY: Yeah. Or at least if you were standing next to the**
26  **pantry you could toss me some chips or something.**
27  **SIERRA: What are we going to do?**

1  MOLLY: Scream?
2  SIERRA: We already did that when I flipped the kitchen
3      light on and we both saw *the stupid scorpion!*
4  MOLLY: I meant scream for help.
5  SIERRA: And who's going to hear us?
6  MOLLY: A neighbor?
7  SIERRA: I doubt that. Too bad I left my cell phone in my
8      bedroom.
9  MOLLY: I left mine in there, too.
10 SIERRA: *Go away!* (Suddenly both GIRLS jump and scream as
11     they look at the floor.)
12 MOLLY: It moved!
13 SIERRA: Not enough. I wish it would turn and walk out the
14     back door.
15 MOLLY: Do you think it knows how?
16 SIERRA: No. I think it's dumb and lost *and needs to die.*
17 MOLLY: Sierra, we can't stand on these chairs all night.
18 SIERRA: Then what are we supposed to do?
19 MOLLY: Kill it.
20 SIERRA: How? Me? You?
21 MOLLY: You.
22 SIERRA: I'm not getting anywhere near that scorpion.
23 MOLLY: Well, I'm not either.
24 SIERRA: Then that means we're stuck.
25 MOLLY: And we have to stand here all night?
26 SIERRA: Unless it leaves.
27 MOLLY: And it doesn't seem interested in doing that, does
28     it?
29 SIERRA: I know. Let's see if we can scare it.
30 MOLLY: How?
31 SIERRA: Let's scream and see it if gets scared and crawls
32     away.
33 MOLLY: I thought we have been screaming.
34 SIERRA: Well, let's try it again. Let's do it on purpose this
35     time and see if we can scare him away.

1   **MOLLY: OK.**

2   **SIERRA: Ready?** *(GIRLS scream. A short pause.)* **Nothing.**

3   **MOLLY: I think it yawned.**

4   **SIERRA: No it didn't. It's not doing anything.**

5   **MOLLY: Have any other great ideas?**

6   **SIERRA: No.** *(Opens book.)* **I guess we can study.**

7   **MOLLY: Like this?**

8   **SIERRA: I don't think we have a choice. I can quiz you for**

9      **the science test. That's what we were going to do**

10     **anyway.**

11  **MOLLY: While eating chips and dip. Not standing over a**

12     **nasty scorpion.**

13  **SIERRA: Well, I don't see that we have another choice.**

14     **Question one.**

15  **MOLLY: Really? We're really going to study for our science**

16     **test like this?**

17  **SIERRA: Question one. What is the temperature of boiling**

18     **water?**

19  **MOLLY: Really? We're actually going to do this?**

20  **SIERRA: You did come over to my house to study. There's**

21     **nothing else to do at the moment. Good thing I**

22     **accidentally carried my science book into the kitchen.**

23     **So, question number one. What is the temperature of**

24     **boiling water?**

25  **MOLLY: Sierra, I can't think clearly with that scorpion**

26     **staring at us.**

27  **SIERRA: Molly, I don't think he's staring at us. I think he's**

28     **sleeping. You're the one who said you saw him yawn. At**

29     **least we can get prepared for this science test while we**

30     **stand here.**

31  **MOLLY: I'm tired of standing here. My feet hurt.**

32  **SIERRA: Are you going to answer the question? What is the**

33     **temperature of —**

34  **MOLLY:** *(Interrupts.)* **Boiling water. I think it's a hundred**

35     **degrees.**

1  SIERRA: Correct! I'd let you ask me a question, but I'm the
2      one who has the book. Next question. True or false.
3  MOLLY: *(Staring at the scorpion)* True.
4  SIERRA: Can I read the question first?
5  MOLLY: False.
6  SIERRA: Molly!
7  MOLLY: What?
8  SIERRA: I haven't even asked the question yet. True or false:
9      Temperature is dependent upon the quantity of matter
10     present.
11 MOLLY: Uh ... it's dependent on what?
12 SIERRA: Upon the quantity of matter present.
13 MOLLY: *(Staring at the scorpion)* Scorpions?
14 SIERRA: No, temperature!
15 MOLLY: *(Looks at SIERRA.)* I don't know what you just asked
16     me. *(Looks back at the scorpion. She screams.)* It moved
17     again!
18 SIERRA: *(Hugging her book)* It moved towards us!
19 MOLLY: I think it wants to bite us. Or eat us. Or something
20     like that.
21 SIERRA: Don't say that.
22 MOLLY: Then let's change the subject. Let's talk about
23     something else. Temperature! Is it dependent on what?
24 SIERRA: *(Opens book, her hands shaking.)* Question two is
25     true or false.
26 MOLLY: True!
27 SIERRA: Let me ask the question first. True or false:
28     Temperature is dependent upon the quantity of matter
29     present.
30 MOLLY: True. I think. I don't know! I can't think because of
31     you-know-what down there who wants to do you-know-
32     what to us.
33 SIERRA: False.
34 MOLLY: Like I said, Sierra, I can't think.
35 SIERRA: Next question.

1   MOLLY: Sierra, I can't do this.

2   ERIN: *(From Off-Stage)* Hello? Hello? Are you guys here?
3       *(Enters the kitchen.)* Hey! Why are you two standing on
4       chairs?

5   SIERRA: Erin, there's a scorpion on the floor!

6   ERIN: *(Jumps onto a nearby chair.)* Oh my gosh! I hate those
7       things.

8   MOLLY: So do we.

9   ERIN: I was driving by on my way to Christy's and thought
10      I'd stop by and say hello.

11  SIERRA: Hi.

12  MOLLY: Hi.

13  ERIN: Hi. How long have you two been up here?

14  MOLLY: It seems like forever.

15  SIERRA: We came into the kitchen to get a snack, turned on
16      the light, and saw it.

17  MOLLY: Screamed bloody murder and jumped onto these
18      chairs. Too bad you didn't come here to save us.

19  ERIN: I just came by to say hello.

20  MOLLY: It looks like we'll be up here all night.

21  SIERRA: Unless it decides *to go away!*

22  ERIN: All night? But I was supposed to go to Christy's to
23      study.

24  SIERRA: Go ahead, but on your way out could you please
25      step on it or smash it with something? Maybe a pot or
26      pan? Or there's a flyswatter on top of the fridge.

27  ERIN: Not me! I hate scorpions. Couldn't we call someone?

28  MOLLY: We left our phones in the bedroom. But did you
29      bring yours, Erin?

30  ERIN: No. I left mine in the car. I saw the front door open
31      and I was just going to drop by and say hello.

32  SIERRA: Well, hello!

33  MOLLY: We were trying to study for the science test when
34      you came in. I was having trouble concentrating,
35      though.

1 ERIN: Wow. There has to be something we can do.

2 SIERRA: If you think of it, let us know.

3 MOLLY: *(Looking up)* I know. Maybe I could jump high
4     enough to grab hold of the kitchen light and swing onto
5     the counter. Then I could crawl to the edge of the
6     counter and jump off into the living room and run next
7     door and call nine-one-one.

8 ERIN: Why wouldn't you just run into the bedroom and
9     grab your cell phone? I don't think the scorpion is that
10     fast.

11 MOLLY: Good point. I'll jump from the kitchen counter into
12     the living room and run to the bedroom, grab my cell
13     phone, and dial nine-one-one.

14 SIERRA: First of all, I think it would be all right to call your
15     dad instead of calling nine-one-one. And second of all,
16     you're not swinging from the kitchen light to the
17     counter because my mom would kill us if you broke it.
18     *And* if you broke it and you fell onto the floor –

19 MOLLY: That thing would eat me alive.

20 ERIN: This is crazy. Look at us. We're humongous compared
21     to that tiny little thing.

22 SIERRA: You're right, Erin. So why don't you jump down
23     there and kill him?

24 ERIN: I would, but I'm afraid of scorpions.

25 MOLLY: So are we.

26 ERIN: But it just seems ridiculous.

27 SIERRA: Yes it does. Which means we've got to think of
28     something to get out of this situation. Minus swinging
29     from the kitchen light and falling on top of those eager
30     pinchers.

31 MOLLY: Believe me, Sierra, I no longer want to jump up and
32     swing from your kitchen light. *(To ERIN)* We tried
33     screaming at him to scare him off, but it didn't work.

34 ERIN: Well, I say whoever is the closest to it needs to spit on
35     it.

1   SIERRA: What?

2   ERIN: Spit on it. Maybe that'll make him scurry along.

3   MOLLY: Well, Erin, that would be you. You're the closest. So
4       go ahead. Spit on him.

5   ERIN: *(Tries, but then turns her head away.)* I'm sorry. I can't.

6   SIERRA: Next great idea?

7   MOLLY: *(Claps her hands.)* Go, go, go! You heard me, go on!

8   ERIN: *(After a pause)* So much for that.

9   SIERRA: *(Opens her book.)* Question number three. What
10      are three elements that can ward off disease in plants?

11  MOLLY: Sierra, do we have to do this right now?

12  ERIN: Is that one of the questions on the test? Gosh, I need
13      to study.

14  MOLLY: Looks like we might have all night to study.

15  ERIN: Three elements to ward off disease? Did we even
16      study this in class?

17  MOLLY: I think we were expected to read it and know it.

18  ERIN: Well, I guess I need to crack open that science book
19      more often. Well, let's see if I can guess. Three elements
20      to ward off disease. *(To MOLLY)* Do you know it?

21  MOLLY: I don't have a clue. But I'm all for guessing.

22  ERIN: Plants need soil ... so soil!

23  SIERRA: Wrong.

24  MOLLY: Water.

25  SIERRA: Correct.

26  ERIN: Water, OK. Uh ... fertilizer.

27  SIERRA: Wrong.

28  MOLLY: Light?

29  SIERRA: Correct.

30  ERIN: Well, surely I can guess this last one. Water, light ...
31      water, light, and ... love!

32  SIERRA: *Wrong!*

33  MOLLY: Air?

34  SIERRA: Correct.

35  ERIN: So it's water, light, and air. Well, I bet I remember that

1      one if it's on the test.

2   SIERRA: Question number four.

3   MOLLY: Sierra, I think you need to be tested, too.

4   SIERRA: Well, I'm the one who has the book.

5   MOLLY: So, toss it here and I'll ask the next question.

6   SIERRA: OK. *(Tosses the book to MOLLY, but MOLLY misses*

7       *and it lands on the floor. The GIRLS scream.)*

8   ERIN: It landed on the scorpion!

9   MOLLY: You killed it, Sierra. You killed it!

10  ERIN: Why didn't we think of this earlier?

11  SIERRA: My book! It's going to have scorpion guts all over it.

12  ERIN: At least it's dead now.

13  MOLLY: Unless it lived through that. Do you think it did?

14  SIERRA: I don't know. Those scorpions are pretty tough

15      little creatures.

16  ERIN: What if it starts to crawl out from under the book?

17  SIERRA: Well, I say we run for it before it has a chance to

18      crawl out.

19  MOLLY: Me too.

20  ERIN: I'm ready.

21  SIERRA: OK, on the count of three, we run out of here as

22      fast as we can. Erin, you can run back out to your car

23      and go to Christy's, and Molly, you and I will run to my

24      bedroom slam the door, put dirty clothes across the

25      bottom of the door, and call my Uncle Bob.

26  MOLLY: OK.

27  ERIN: On the count of three ...

28  SIERRA: One ... two ... three! *(GIRLS jump down and run Off-*

29      *Stage screaming.)*

# 24. The Worst Speech Class Ever

CAST: (3M, 5F) MRS. DAVIS, ISABEL, LESLIE, KYLE,
AMANDA, LUKE, MARIA, CHAD
PROPS: Notebook paper, 3 x 5 index cards
SETTING: Classroom

1   *(At rise, ISABEL stands nervously in front of the "class."*
2   *She holds a single piece of notebook paper, which shakes*
3   *in her hands at times. MRS. DAVIS stands to the side to*
4   *offer advice and criticism. Note: It is always just MRS.*
5   *DAVIS and the student giving the speech. All others wait*
6   *Off-Stage until their turn.)*
7  **MRS. DAVIS: All right class, Isabel will be the first student to**
8   **give her speech. Some last minute reminders: eye**
9   **contact, don't fidget, and speak loud and clearly so the**
10  **audience can hear you. And as I told you at the**
11  **beginning of the school year, you will be graded on**
12  **each and every speech you perform, so let me see your**
13  **very best. And I know we've talked about this before,**
14  **but what is the number one fear of all people?** *(Pause)*
15  **Anyone?** *(Pause)* **Well, we know that the second fear to**
16  **all humans is death. So what is the number one fear of**
17  **all people?** *(Pause, then claps her hands together.)* **Come**
18  **on! You know this! Public speaking is the number one**
19  **fear. Yes, that's right. Death is the second fear and**
20  **public speaking is first. So what does this mean? It**
21  **means giving speeches is more fearful than death. And**
22  **that, students, is something that you will overcome in**
23  **my class.** *(To ISABEL)* **Go ahead, Isabel.**
24 **ISABEL:** *(Glances at the sheet of notebook paper, her hands*
25   *shaking. She speaks very softly.)* **This is about my**
26   **favorite season of the year. My favorite season of the**
27   **year is —**

1   **MRS. DAVIS:** **Louder, please.**

2   **ISABEL:** *(Continues to speak softly.)* **My favorite season of the**
3       **year is summer. Why, you might ask? Well, it's because**
4       **of many reasons. Here's my list. Number one, it's not**
5       **cold.**

6   **MRS. DAVIS:** **Stop! Isabel, the class cannot hear you. Class,**
7       **can you hear Isabel?** *(Pause)* **They cannot. Start again,**
8       **please.**

9   **ISABEL: Mrs. Davis, do I have to read this out loud?**

10   **MRS. DAVIS:** **No, you don't have to read it out loud, Isabel.**
11       **That's because it's a speech and you don't read**
12       **speeches. Start again, please.**

13   **ISABEL:** *(Stares at the sheet of notebook paper, attempting to*
14       *speak louder, but can't seem to.)* **My favorite season of**
15       **the year is summer. Why, you might ask? Well, it's**
16       **because of many reasons. Here's my list. Number one,**
17       **it's not cold —**

18   **MRS. DAVIS:** **Stop! Please, stop. Isabel, we cannot hear a**
19       **word you are saying. And if we can't hear a word you**
20       **are saying, what is the point in standing up here and**
21       **giving a speech?**

22   **ISABEL: I guess I'm nervous, Mrs. Davis.**

23   **MRS. DAVIS:** **Sit down.** *(ISABEL exits.)* **Leslie, would you**
24       **please come up here and show Isabel how to properly**
25       **give a speech.**

26   **LESLIE:** *(Enters carrying a single index card. She clears her*
27       *throat.)* **How many months contain twenty-eight days?**
28       *(Pause)* **All twelve!**

29   **MRS. DAVIS:** **Good, Leslie. Class, beginning a speech with a**
30       **joke will immediately grab your audience's attention.**
31       **Good, Leslie. Go on.**

32   **LESLIE: Christmas is the season of all seasons. Yes,**
33       **Christmas is my favorite season.**

34   **MRS. DAVIS: Leslie, Christmas is not a season.**

35   **LESLIE: Yes it is. That's why we say it's the Christmas**
36       **season.**

1  **MRS. DAVIS: I asked you to prepare a speech regarding your**
2      **favorite season. Spring, summer, fall, or winter. And**
3      **Christmas is not one of the four seasons.**
4  **LESLIE: It's not?**
5  **MRS. DAVIS: No.**
6  **LESLIE: But my speech is on the Christmas season.**
7  **MRS. DAVIS: Sit down, Leslie. Maybe after Isabel finds her**
8      **voice and nerves to give her speech, you can present a**
9      **new one — on one of the four seasons!**
10 **LESLIE: Yes ma'am.** *(Exits.)*
11 **MRS. DAVIS: Kyle, would you like to go next?**
12 **KYLE:** *(Enters.)* **I guess.** *(He glances down at the palm of his*
13     *hand.)* **The season I like best is ...** *(Looks at his hand)*
14     **summer.** *(To ISABEL)* **Hey Isabel, we picked the same**
15     **season.**
16 **MRS. DAVIS: Continue, Kyle.**
17 **KYLE:** *(Looks at his hand.)* **OK. So my favorite season of the**
18     **year is winter.**
19 **MRS. DAVIS: Kyle, you just said it was summer.**
20 **KYLE: Oh yeah!** *(Looks at hand.)* **Yeah, my favorite season is**
21     **summer.** *(Looks at the palm of his other hand.)* **And**
22     **those reasons are ...** *(Reading off his hand)* **no school,**
23     **swimming, watermelon, Fourth of July, vacations, no**
24     **school, and ... and I can't read the last one. I think I**
25     **sweated if off.**
26 **MRS. DAVIS:** *(Looks at the palms of his hands.)* **Kyle, what is**
27     **this?**
28 **KYLE: Notes for my speech. See, the last one smeared off. I**
29     **got sweaty.**
30 **MRS. DAVIS: Did I not tell you that you were allowed an**
31     **index card for your notes?**
32 **KYLE: Yeah, but I didn't have any. So ...** *(Shrugs.)*
33 **MRS. DAVIS: Sit down, Kyle. Is there anyone in this room**
34     **who is prepared to give their speech?** *(Pause)* **Amanda?**
35 **AMANDA:** *(Enters. She speaks very fast, so fast you can hardly*

1     *understand what she is saying.)* **My absolute favorite**
2     **season of the year is Christmas because it's in the**
3     **winter. I mean my absolute favorite season of the year**
4     **is winter because Christmas is in winter. And**
5     **Christmas is full of wonderful things. Family, friends,**
6     **food. Giving presents. Opening presents. Santa Claus**
7     **and Rudolph the Red-Nosed Reindeer. If you still**
8     **believe in those things. I do and I hope I always believe**
9     **in Santa. Because believing in Santa is what makes**
10     **Christmas Christmas.**
11 **MRS. DAVIS: Amanda, slow down. We can't understand a**
12     **word you are saying.** *(Mimics AMANDA by speaking*
13     *fast.)* **Can you understand what I'm saying when I talk**
14     **this fast? Can you? Can you understand me at all? If you**
15     **can't, it's because I'm talking a mile a minute and it**
16     **sounds absolutely horrid, doesn't it? Is that the way you**
17     **want to sound, Amanda? Horrid?**
18 **AMANDA: What did you say?**
19 **MRS. DAVIS: I said to slow down.**
20 **AMANDA: Can I start over?**
21 **MRS. DAVIS: Last chance, Amanda.**
22 **AMANDA:** *(Speaks very, very slowly.)* **My absolute favorite**
23     **season of the year is Christmas because it's in the**
24     **winter. I mean my absolute favorite season of the year**
25     **is winter because Christmas is in winter —**
26 **MRS. DAVIS:** *(Interrupting)* **You're putting me to sleep,**
27     **Amanda.**
28 **AMANDA: What? I'm putting you to sleep?**
29 **MRS. DAVIS:** *(Mimics her by speaking slowly.)* **When you talk**
30     **like this you put me to sleep. Sit down, Amanda.**
31     *(AMANDA exits.)* **Is anyone, anyone at all, prepared to**
32     **give his or her speech?** *(Pause)* **Anyone?** *(Pause)* **Then**
33     **Luke, you are next.**
34 **LUKE:** *(From Off-Stage)* **Ah, man!**
35 **MRS. DAVIS: Are you ready, Luke?**

1   LUKE: *(Enters.)* I guess.

2   MRS. DAVIS: All right, then. Proceed.

3   LUKE: My favorite season is Halloween because that's when
4   I get to —

5   MRS. DAVIS: Halloween is not a season!

6   LUKE: Yes it is.

7   MRS. DAVIS: No it's not.

8   LUKE: Uh-huh! Because we decorate my house and I put on
9   this scary devil costume and jump out of the bushes
10   and scare the little kids when they come to the door to
11   say trick or treat. *(Laughs.)* And the little kids scream
12   and run away crying for their moms. And then I eat the
13   candy on the ground that they dropped out of their
14   Halloween buckets and then —

15   MRS. DAVIS: Sit down, Luke. *(LUKE exits.)* Maria, you are
16   next. Please, show the class how a speech is to be
17   presented. Please.

18   MARIA: *(Enters holding a large stack of index cards. As she*
19   *speaks, she constantly flips through the cards.)* Spring is
20   my season of choice. *(Flips.)* Refreshing. *(Flips.)*
21   Thawing. *(Flips.)* Warm. *(Flips.)* Flowers blooming.
22   *(Flips.)* Birds singing. *(Flips.)* Rain showers. *(Flips.)* And
23   my birthday. *(Flips.)*

24   MRS. DAVIS: That is not a speech.

25   MARIA: But I wasn't finished. *(Flips through cards.)* Spring is
26   like a breath of fresh air. *(Flips.)* A time for new
27   beginnings. *(Flips.)* The end of winter and beginning of
28   spring. *(Flips.)* Spring alive! *(Flips.)* Spring is here!

29   MRS. DAVIS: Sit down. That was terrible. *(MARIA exits.)*

30   CHAD: *(Enters.)* I'll go next.

31   MRS. DAVIS: Whatever.

32   CHAD: *(In a confident tone)* Thank you very much for
33   inviting me. And, to Mrs. Davis, thank you for teaching
34   this class and instructing us on the art of giving
35   speeches. It's always a pleasure to present the great

1    lessons we have learned from your class. Today, the
2    four seasons of our year are to be explored. What we
3    once experienced as distinct and noticeable changes as
4    each season came upon us is slowly dissolving to the
5    point of a one-for-all season. If I might explain, a season
6    with no substantial changes. You move from one to the
7    other with no change of forecast. Gone are the days of
8    cold climates, snow falling from the sky, and the cold
9    brutal wind. And why? Why has this cold temperature
10   disappeared? The cold temperature that sustains our
11   polar bears and penguins and other Arctic animals is
12   disappearing. Global change. Global warming! It's
13   coming to a world near you.
14  MRS. DAVIS: Chad. Did I ask for a speech on global
15   warming?
16  CHAD: Mrs. Davis, you asked for a speech on the four
17   seasons.
18  MRS. DAVIS: Your favorite season.
19  CHAD: Mrs. Davis, if global warming continues at this rate,
20   there will no longer be four seasons.
21  MRS. DAVIS: Chad, sit down.
22  CHAD: But —
23  MRS. DAVIS: Sit down. *(CHAD exits. She paces back and forth*
24   *for a moment as she gathers her thoughts.)* Let me just
25   say this. This is the worst speech class ever. Ever! In all
26   my years of instructing students to give speeches, this
27   is by far the worst. So what does that mean? It means
28   it's back to square one. Back to the basics for you young
29   people in here. So open your speech book to page one.
30   Yes, that's right, page one. *(Pause)* And let me remind
31   you, public speaking is the number one fear of all
32   people. Second to death! And if you are wondering how
33   giving speeches is more fearful than death, well, let me
34   enlighten you, you speechless students out there! Why?
35   Because you are scared to stand in front of your peers

1        **because you might sound like an idiot. And did you**

2        **sound like an idiot today? Did you? Well, let me answer**

3        **that question for you. Yes! Yes you did! Yes, yes, yes!**

# 25. Paper Airplanes

CAST: (3M) CARLOS, ADAM, MR. COLE
PROPS: Paper, pens
SETTING: Classroom

1  *(At rise, CARLOS is sitting at a desk writing.)*
2  **CARLOS: I will not throw paper airplanes across the room**
3      **during class. I will not throw paper airplanes across**
4      **the room during class. I will not throw —**
5  **ADAM:** *(Enters.)* **Hey. What's going on?**
6  **CARLOS: Hey. Writing "I will not throw paper airplanes**
7      **across the room during class" five hundred times.**
8  **ADAM: Why?**
9  **CARLOS: Because I threw paper airplanes across the room**
10     **during class.**
11 **ADAM: Why?**
12 **CARLOS: I like to experiment with aerodynamics. And I was**
13     **trying to hit the back of Mr. Cole's head.**
14 **ADAM: Why?**
15 **CARLOS: It seemed like the thing to do.**
16 **ADAM: So did you hit the back of Mr. Cole's head?**
17 **CARLOS: Almost. Aimed my classic dart airplane right for**
18     **the center of that round bald spot on the back of his**
19     **head, but missed. Hit his ear instead.**
20 **ADAM: How did he know it was you who threw it?**
21 **CARLOS: Oh, because Mr. Cole has eyes in the back of his**
22     **head. At least that's what he said. But I think the truth**
23     **is, Casey Hibblewinkle did this when Mr. Cole turned**
24     **around.** *(Pointing as if tattling on someone)*
25 **ADAM: That Casey Hibblewinkle is a notorious tattletale.**
26     **Last week he told Mrs. Richwood that I was fooling**
27     **around during silent reading time. You know Mrs.**
28     **Richwood likes us to sit in her English class and do**
29     **nothing but read. And I mean nothing else!**

1   CARLOS: What were you doing?

2   ADAM: Eating Doritos. Sneaking them out of my backpack
3      and well, you know those Doritos aren't exactly quiet.
4      And Casey Hibblewinkle said, "Hey, I keep hearing a
5      loud crunch. It's messing up my concentration." And of
6      course Casey Hibblewinkle was staring at me as he
7      made this announcement. And Mrs. Richwood didn't
8      have to look far as I swallowed a half eaten chip. Gulp!
9      She marched over to my desk and confiscated my
10     Doritos and sent me to the office for a little talk with
11     Mrs. Hazekemp. Believe me, I don't bring Doritos to
12     school anymore, thanks to Casey Hibblewinkle.

13   CARLOS: And thanks to Casey Hibblewinkle, my hand is
14     going to fall off by the time I write this sentence five
15     hundred times. *(Writing)* I will not throw paper
16     airplanes across the room during class.

17   ADAM: And Mr. Cole's bald spot on his head was such a good
18     target, too.

19   CARLOS: I know. *(Jumps up and draws a circle on the*
20     *blackboard.)* I think I'll practice. See that circle on the
21     board? I'm going to pretend that's the back of Mr. Cole's
22     bald head. *(Starts making a paper airplane.)* So what are
23     you doing here?

24   ADAM: Mr. Cole said he wanted to see me.

25   CARLOS: Uh-oh. Do you have any idea why?

26   ADAM: I have a very good idea why. Yesterday I thought it
27     would be funny if I clapped out loud every time Mr.
28     Cole finished talking. *(Demonstrates.)* The American
29     Civil War was a civil war within the United States.
30     *(Claps loudly.)* The Civil War lasted from 1861 to 1865.
31     *(Claps loudly.)* The war was long and bloody. *(Claps*
32     *loudly.)* The South was devastated. *(Claps loudly.)*
33     General Lee surrendered to General Grant on April
34     ninth, 1865. *(Claps loudly.)* The war was over. *(Claps.)*
35     Bravo! Bravo!

1   CARLOS: That's funny. What did Mr. Cole say about you
2      clapping during his Civil War lecture?
3   ADAM: Oh, nothing. But he glared at me the entire time.
4      Then during my homeroom class this morning I
5      received a note that said he wanted to see me.
6   CARLOS: You're dead.
7   ADAM: I know. Hey, maybe Mr. Cole will ask me to write "I
8      will not clap during class" five hundred times.
9   CARLOS: Maybe. Last week he made Megan write "I will not
10     sleep and snore loudly in class." I think Megan was
11     faking it as a dare, but she still got into trouble with Mr.
12     Cole.
13   ADAM: Well, beats detention.
14   CARLOS: True. And if I can skip detention and sit in his
15     class during his off period and write a sentence five
16     hundred times, I'd say flying paper airplanes was
17     worth it. I do it in my other classes and never get
18     caught.
19   ADAM: Because Casey Hibblewinkle isn't in your classes to
20     tattletale on you.
21   CARLOS: OK, here it goes. *(Throws his paper airplane.)* Close.
22     But I'll keep trying. *(Makes more paper airplanes and*
23     *continues to throw them.)*
24   ADAM: Wonder where Mr. Cole is?
25   CARLOS: Beats me. But if he comes in here and wonders
26     why I've written "I will not throw paper airplanes
27     across the room in class" only twenty times, I'll tell him
28     I write very slowly. *(Throws another paper airplane.)* Ah,
29     that was close! I'm going to keep trying until I hit my
30     target of Mr. Cole's bald spot.
31   ADAM: Let me have some paper. I want to try. *(Takes paper*
32     *from CARLOS.)* I bet I can hit Mr. Cole's bald spot. *(For a*
33     *few minutes, CARLOS and ADAM make paper airplanes*
34     *and throw them at a target on a board. All of a sudden,*
35     *MR. COLE enters the room just as the boys*

1      simultaneously throw a paper airplane his direction.)
2   CARLOS: Uh-oh.
3   ADAM: This is not good.
4   MR. COLE: What is this?
5   CARLOS: I ... was ... uh ... practicing what you told me not to
6       do during class.
7   ADAM: Getting it out of his system.
8   CARLOS: Yeah!
9   ADAM: I was helping him.
10  MR. COLE: Could you boys be any more immature in your
11      behavior?
12  CARLOS: Yes sir. I mean, no sir.
13  ADAM: No sir. Or were we supposed to say yes sir? I'm
14      confused. Could you repeat the question, Mr. Cole?
15  MR. COLE: Paper airplanes. Did we not do that in fifth
16      grade?
17  ADAM: I didn't.
18  CARLOS: Me neither.
19  MR. COLE: And do you think it's appropriate behavior for
20      high school? At your ages?
21  ADAM: No sir.
22  CARLOS: No sir.
23  MR. COLE: Carlos, how are you coming along with your
24      sentences?
25  CARLOS: Uh ... (Looking at his paper) Coming right along, sir.
26  MR. COLE: Are you almost finished writing your sentence
27      five hundred times?
28  CARLOS: Uh ...
29  MR. COLE: Where are you?
30  CARLOS: (Quietly) Twenty.
31  MR. COLE: What? I can't hear you.
32  CARLOS: Twenty.
33  MR. COLE: Twenty? That's it?
34  CARLOS: Yes sir.
35  MR. COLE: And do you know what's sad?

1 CARLOS: Yes sir. I mean, no sir.
2 MR. COLE: What's sad is that for throwing paper airplanes
3     when I told you not to throw paper airplanes is going to
4     cost you. And do you know what it's going to cost you?
5 CARLOS: More sentences?
6 MR. COLE: More sentences. One thousand sentences. Every
7     day you show up in my class during my off period so I
8     can watch you write out one thousand times, "I
9     promise I will not throw paper airplanes across the
10     room during class."
11 CARLOS: Uh, Mr. Cole —
12 MR. COLE: One thousand times, Carlos!
13 CARLOS: I don't mean to argue with you, but you told me to
14     write, "I will not throw paper airplanes across the
15     room during class." But just now you added "*I promise
16     I will not throw paper airplanes across the room
17     during class.*" That's the first time I've heard about the
18     promise part.
19 MR. COLE: You didn't write "I promise" in your sentences?
20 CARLOS: No sir.
21 MR. COLE: Well, then it looks like you'll need to start all
22     over, doesn't it?
23 CARLOS: But ... couldn't I just like write really, really small
24     and add "I promise" to the first twenty sentences?
25 MR. COLE: Carlos.
26 CARLOS: Sir?
27 MR. COLE: Let me see your paper. *(Takes CARLOS' paper and*
28     *crumples it.)* No! You need to start over.
29 CARLOS: Yes sir. *(Begins writing. Mumbling as he writes)* I
30     promise I will not to throw paper airplanes across the
31     room during class.
32 MR. COLE: Quiet, please. Now to you, Adam.
33 ADAM: Yes sir.
34 MR. COLE: Tell me what you learned in our study about the
35     Civil War.

1  ADAM: What I learned?

2  MR. COLE: What you learned, Adam.

3  ADAM: Well ... I learned ... the American Civil War was a civil
4      war within the United States. *(MR COLE claps loudly.)*
5      And the uh ... Civil War lasted from 1861 to 1865. *(MR.*
6      *COLE claps loudly.)* The war was uh ... long and bloody.
7      *(MR. COLE claps loudly.)* The ... uh ... south was
8      devastated. *(MR. COLE claps loudly.)* And uh ... General
9      Lee surrendered to General Grant on April ninth, 1865.
10     *(MR. COLE claps loudly.)* The war was over. *(MR. COLE*
11     *claps.)*

12  MR. COLE: Bravo! Bravo! Now let me tell you what you are
13     going to write, Adam. For acting like a smart aleck in
14     class and clapping, you will write "I will not clap
15     during class when Mr. Cole is teaching" five hundred
16     times.

17  ADAM: Yes sir.

18  MR. COLE: *And* for throwing paper airplanes, you will write
19     "I promise I will not throw paper airplanes across the
20     room during class" five hundred times. So, it looks like
21     the two of you have a lot of writing to do. One thousand
22     sentences!

23  ADAM: Yes sir.

24  CARLOS: Yes sir.

25  MR. COLE: *(Laughing)* One thousand sentences! That'll
26     teach you boys. *(He exits.)*

27  CARLOS: Can you believe him?

28  ADAM: I'm going to develop carpal tunnel.

29  CARLOS: I think I already have.

30  ADAM: We'll be in this class for a hundred years.

31  CARLOS: Why can't we just type it on the computer? Who
32     ever writes out anything these days?

33  ADAM: I know. Probably because Mr. Cole thinks we'd just
34     copy and paste.

35  CARLOS: I would.

1  **ADAM: Me too.**

2  **CARLOS:** *(Speaks as he writes.)* ***I promise*** **I will not throw**
3      **paper airplanes across the room during class.**

4  **ADAM:** *(Speaks as he writes.)* **I will not clap during class**
5      **when Mr. Cole is teaching.**

6  **CARLOS:** *(Speaks as he writes.)* ***I promise*** **I will not throw**
7      **paper airplanes across the room during class.**

8  **ADAM:** *(Speaks as he writes.)* **I will not clap during class**
9      **when Mr. Cole is teaching.**

10  **CARLOS: Writing all these sentences makes me want to**
11      **throw a paper airplane at his head.**

12  **ADAM: And it makes me want to clap.**

13  **CARLOS: And he's not here, so you know what? I'm going to**
14      **throw one more paper airplane ... maybe my last ... at**
15      **my target. Mr. Cole's bald spot!** *(Makes an airplane.)*

16  **ADAM: Do it! He's not here. Make it good if it's your last.**

17  **CARLOS:** *(Mumbling as he makes his airplane)* **One thousand**
18      **sentences! How stupid is that? Talk about immature.**
19      **Whoever heard of teachers making you write out**
20      **sentences as a punishment? Maybe in first grade, but in**
21      **high school?**

22  **ADAM: I'm with you, man.** *(MR. COLE enters as the following*
23      *happens.)*

24  **CARLOS: My target ... Mr. Cole's bald spot!** *(Throws the*
25      *airplane. ADAM claps loudly. Suddenly they both see MR.*
26      *COLE. They quickly go back to their writing.)*

27  **CARLOS:** *(Speaks as he writes.)* **I promise I will not throw**
28      **paper airplanes across the room during class.**

29  **ADAM:** *(Speaks as he writes.)* **I will not clap during class**
30      **when Mr. Cole is teaching. Or not teaching. Or ever,**
31      **ever again.**

# 26. Intervention

CAST: (2M, 2F) JOSH, MASON, TORI, ARIANA
PROPS: Cell phone
SETTING: Mason's house

1  *(At rise, MASON, TORI, and ARIANA are sitting in a room*
2  *when JOSH enters.)*
3  **JOSH:** *(Enters the room and looks around.)* **What is this?**
4  **MASON: Josh, we all want to talk to you.**
5  **JOSH: Mason, I came over because I thought you and I were**
6  **going to play some basketball. Are we all going to play?**
7  **MASON: No.**
8  **JOSH: Then what's going on?**
9  **TORI: Mason, lock the door.** *(MASON locks the door.)*
10  **ARIANA: Josh, we're all your friends, you know that, don't**
11  **you?**
12  **JOSH: What's going on?**
13  **TORI: Josh, this is an intervention.**
14  **JOSH: It is? For who? Ariana? Mason? I know it's not for me.**
15  **I know! It's for Ariana's obsession with *Harry Potter.***
16  **Reading those books over and over and over again.**
17  **Those posters all over her room. The *Harry Potter* chat**
18  **rooms. The blogs. Naming her new puppy Harry Potter.**
19  **The *Harry Potter* games. The framed autograph from**
20  **J.K. Rowling. Starting her own *Harry Potter* fan club.**
21  **Dressing up like Harry Potter and going to the**
22  **bookstore for the midnight release. Yes, I'm in. Ariana,**
23  **this fantasy world that you are living in has got to stop.**
24  **ARIANA: Josh, I'm so over *Harry Potter.***
25  **JOSH: You are?**
26  **ARIANA: Let me just say that I'm able to have a life beyond**
27  ***Harry Potter.* Don't get me wrong, I still love him, but I**
28  **have other things I'm interested in.**
29  **JOSH: Well, good. Then that means it's you, Tori. This**

1      intervention is for you. And I know why.

2  TORI: You do? Well, please, tell me why you think it's for me.

3  JOSH: You collect boyfriends like Ariana collects *Harry*
4      *Potter* memorabilia.

5  TORI: Excuse me?

6  JOSH: In the past month you have gone out with Andrew,
7      Caleb, Hunter, Kevin, Isaac, Danny, Bryan, Bryan
8      number two, and Aaron. Girl, you have got a problem.

9  TORI: I do not. I liked them for a few days and then I didn't.
10     So I broke up with them.

11  JOSH: Because you're afraid of commitment. Right?

12  TORI: No! Because I just stopped liking them. Call me picky.

13  JOSH: No. I think you're trying to find your self-worth
14     through boyfriends.

15  TORI: I am not! I just stopped liking them. Andrew was
16     controlling, Caleb was into sports more than he was
17     into me, Hunter was two-timing me, Kevin had no
18     personality, Isaac couldn't remember my name, Danny
19     constantly wrote me long love letters that I didn't have
20     time to read, Bryan number one was rude to people,
21     and Bryan number two had no sense of style.

22  JOSH: And Aaron?

23  TORI: I'm still with Aaron. One week, going on one week
24     and a day, thank you very much.

25  JOSH: But you'll kick him to the curb by tomorrow, won't
26     you?

27  TORI: No!

28  JOSH: Because you can't be happy with anyone. Isn't that
29     right?

30  TORI: That's not true.

31  JOSH: Come on, people. Let's tell Tori how she finds fault in
32     everyone. Collects boyfriends like bubblegum, chews
33     them up and then spits them out.

34  TORI: You're wrong! This intervention is not about me. I
35     love Aaron and I'm staying with him.

1   JOSH: Then if it's not about Ariana and her *Harry Potter*
2       obsession or you with your boyfriend issues ... Ah-ha!
3       It's my buddy Mason over here. Oh yes, and I know
4       exactly why. I'm here for you, my friend.
5   MASON: You think it's about me?
6   JOSH: Of course.
7   MASON: Why?
8   JOSH: Don't be embarrassed.
9   MASON: I'm not.
10   JOSH: We are here to help you get past this.
11   MASON: Get past what?
12   JOSH: You know.
13   MASON: No I don't.
14   JOSH: I guess the first step is saying it out loud, isn't it
15       people?
16   ARIANA: I'd like to hear this.
17   TORI: Me too.
18   JOSH: Mason, you have low self-esteem.
19   MASON: That's not true.
20   JOSH: How many times have I heard you say "I'm stupid" or,
21       "I can't do this"?
22   MASON: Calculus, dude. It's hard.
23   JOSH: I'm stupid. I'm so stupid.
24   MASON: When it comes to calculus.
25   JOSH: And you wouldn't ask Brittany out.
26   MASON: Because I'm too ugly for Brittany.
27   JOSH: See! Low self-esteem. No self-confidence at all.
28   MASON: Not when it comes to Brittany. She's like the
29       prettiest girl in the entire universe. She'd never go out
30       with me.
31   JOSH: And I believe you told me you weren't worthy of her.
32   MASON: Well, even if I were, Brittany wouldn't think so.
33   JOSH: And let's move along to the gym.
34   MASON: What? Because I said I felt like Pee Wee Herman
35       standing next to all those body builders? So?

1   JOSH: Mason, it's your negative thoughts that are bringing
2         you down. Right guys? It's OK to strive to improve
3         yourself, but don't criticize yourself for not being
4         perfect.
5   MASON: Josh, did you not feel like Pee Wee Herman when
6         we were standing next to all those college guys with
7         twenty-inch biceps?
8   JOSH: I did not feel like Pee Wee Herman.
9   MASON: Well, good for you, Josh, because I did.
10   JOSH: And today at lunch you said you were an idiot.
11   MASON: For losing my lunch money.
12   JOSH: Again, Mason, the negative talk is bringing you down.
13         You were so depressed all during lunch.
14   MASON: Because I was hungry.
15   JOSH: And let me offer you a little advice, Mr. Stupid, Pee
16         Wee Herman, and Idiotic Person! Negative self-talk is a
17         mixture of half-truths, distortions of reality, and
18         unrealistic logic. Your daily inner dialogue spoken
19         internally or aloud is bringing you down. You need to
20         stop belittling yourself and practice positive thinking.
21         Remind yourself that you are a worthwhile person. Be
22         proud of yourself. Visualize yourself as capable and
23         confident. Acknowledge the things you do well, even if
24         they are small. And allow yourself to make mistakes.
25         But most of all, don't give up! *(Takes a breath.)* OK. Are
26         the rest of you ready to chime in? Tori? Ariana?
27   ARIANA: I'd like to say something.
28   JOSH: *(Puts his arm around MASON.)* Just listen, man. We're
29         all here to help you. Go ahead, Ariana.
30   ARIANA: Josh, this intervention is not for Mason.
31   TORI: It's for you, Josh.
32   JOSH: No it's not. Tori, tell Mason he can overcome his
33         negative self-talk. *(Pats MASON.)* We know you can do
34         this. Try saying this, "I like myself." Three little words,
35         but so powerful. "I like myself." Say it, Mason. "I like
36         myself."

1    MASON: I like myself. Always have, always will.

2    JOSH: Good, good.

3    ARIANA: Josh, look at me. We're all here because of you, not

4        Mason.

5    TORI: That's right. This intervention is for you.

6    MASON: She's telling the truth, Josh.

7    JOSH: *(Takes his hand off MASON.)* I don't believe this. I

8        don't have any problems. At least not any serious

9        enough to warrant an intervention.

10   ARIANA: Yes you do, Josh.

11   TORI: A big problem. Tell him, Mason.

12   MASON: Dude, listen, we're your friends and we want to

13       save you from embarrassing yourself.

14   TORI: Big time.

15   ARIANA: Because a true friend will be honest with you and

16       that's what we're here to do.

17   JOSH: What? What are you guys talking about?

18   MASON: Josh, you can't sing.

19   JOSH: What?

20   ARIANA: Can't carry a tune.

21   TORI: Some people call it tone deaf.

22   JOSH: I'm not tone deaf. I'm in choir at school and at my

23       church. And just last week I entered the school's own

24       version of *American Idol* that's taking place next

25       month. And guess what? They picked me! I'm in. I'm

26       one of the contestants for San Jacinto's *American Idol.*

27   MASON: Josh, do you suppose you were picked because it

28       will make the audience laugh? You know, like on

29       *American Idol* when those people enter the room with

30       all the confidence in the world that they can sing and

31       then they sound horrible. Then the room erupts with

32       laughter. And the audience is laughing their heads off

33       as this person is shocked to hear the judges' comments.

34   ARIANA: Are you bloody kidding me?

35   TORI: What was that?

1   ARIANA: Did you intend to destroy that song?

2   TORI: This is a joke, right?

3   MASON: Let's take a vote.

4   TORI: Josh, I'm sorry, but that was terrible.

5   ARIANA: I'm sorry, Josh. I have to say no.

6   MASON: It's three nos. Sorry, Josh. Off you go.

7   JOSH: Why are you guys doing this to me? You all know I can
8       sing. Is this a joke?

9   MASON: Dude, we're telling you the truth.

10  JOSH: No you're not.

11  TORI: Josh, just because you can't carry a tune doesn't mean
12      we don't love you.

13  JOSH: If I can't carry a tune, then why hasn't my choir
14      teacher at school or church informed me of this?

15  ARIANA: Because they don't hear you on an individual
16      basis. You know, you just blend in with the rest of the
17      singers.

18  JOSH: No! I tried out for the Christmas musical at my
19      church.

20  MASON: And you got a solo?

21  JOSH: No, but I'm one of the eight carolers. And at school I
22      competed in the UIL solo competition.

23  TORI: And?

24  JOSH: And the judge said I was a little off tune. But that was
25      the week I had a sore throat and practically lost my
26      voice.

27  ARIANA: What rank did you get?

28  JOSH: I got fourth place in division, but it's only because my
29      throat hurt.

30  MASON: Josh, I'm telling you the truth. You can't sing.

31  JOSH: Yes I can. *(Bursts out singing very badly. Any song can*
32      *be used.)* I dreamed a dream, in time gone by, when
33      hope was high, and life worth living. *(As JOSH ends the*
34      *song in a dreadful tone, the others cover their ears.)* See.
35      I can sing.

1   TORI: That was painful.

2   ARIANA: Beyond painful.

3   MASON: Excruciating!

4   JOSH: Why are you guys doing this?

5   MASON: We told you, Josh. This is an intervention. And as

6       your friends, we are here to tell you the truth.

7   TORI: You need to face the truth, Josh. You're a horrible

8       singer.

9   ARIANA: Horrible.

10  TORI: But we still love you.

11  ARIANA: But we don't ever want to hear you sing again.

12  TORI: Please.

13  JOSH: No! I want the three of you to sit down and listen. I

14      mean, really listen. And after hearing this, if you really

15      believe I'm terrible at singing, then tell me. *(They sit*

16      *down and JOSH stands in front of them and clears his*

17      *throat. He sings very badly again.)* I dreamed a dream, in

18      time gone by, when hope was high, and life worth

19      living. *(He ends the song in a dreadful tone and the*

20      *others cover their ears.)* Tell me I can't sing.

21  MASON: Josh, you can't sing.

22  TORI: I agree. You can't sing.

23  ARIANA: I'm sorry, Josh, but you can't sing.

24  JOSH: That is such a lie. You know what I'm going to do?

25      *(Picks up a cell phone.)* I'm going to call my choir

26      teacher, Mrs. Riggs, from school. We'll see what she has

27      to say. *(Dials.)* Mrs. Riggs! This is Josh Finder from choir

28      ... No, everything is OK. Mrs. Riggs, I have a huge favor

29      to ask of you. I'm going to sing a song for you and I want

30      you to tell me how I sound. OK? ... Great! Thank you,

31      Mrs. Riggs. Are you ready? *(Sings.)* I dreamed a dream,

32      in time gone by, when hope was high, and life worth

33      living. *(Into the phone)* What? ... It was? ... OK. ... Thanks.

34      *(Hangs up phone.)*

35  ARIANA: What did she say?

1   JOSH: *(Screams.)* Intervention is over!

2   TORI: Why? What happened?

3   MASON: I think he heard the truth from Mrs. Riggs.

4   TORI: Oh.

5   ARIANA: I'm sorry, Josh. But we still love you.

6   JOSH: Mrs. Riggs said it was the most horrific version of "I
7       Dreamed a Dream" she had ever heard.

8   MASON: Don't feel bad, Josh. I can't sing either.

9   TORI: Neither can I.

10  ARIANA: I'm pretty bad myself. I just sing in the shower.

11  JOSH: But I love to sing. In fact, I wanted to be a professional
12      singer.

13  MASON: Well ... be a professional wrestler or something like
14      that. You're young enough to change courses in your
15      life.

16  JOSH: But I dreamed of singing since I was five.

17  TORI: I dreamed of being a dog. But that didn't work out.

18  ARIANA: And I wanted to be a child actress. But that didn't
19      work out either.

20  MASON: There are other things you are good at, Josh.

21  JOSH: Like what?

22  MASON: Like ... uh ...

23  JOSH: It's singing. I love to sing! And you know what? I'm
24      not giving up.

25  TORI: Uh-oh. Don't unlock the door quite yet, Mason.

26  ARIANA: Looks like we're going to be in here for a while.

27  JOSH: I'm never giving up my dream to sing. Never! *(Sings.)*
28      I dreamed a dream, in time gone by, when hope was
29      high, and life worth living.

30  TORI: This is going to be a long night.

31  MASON: Tell me about it.

32  ARIANA: Should we order a pizza?

33  MASON: I think so. *(JOSH continues to sing as they cover their
34      ears and attempt to agree on a type of pizza to order.)*

# About the Author

Laurie Allen was drawn to the theatre while performing plays under the legendary drama instructor, Jerry P. Worsham, at Snyder High School. In this small West Texas town, advancing to and winning the State UIL One-Act Competition in Austin was a goal often achieved. The drama department was hugely supported by the community and earned a reputation of respect and awe as they brought home many awards and first place trophies.

Following this experience, Laurie decided to try her hand at writing plays. Her first play, "Gutter Girl," won the Indian River Players Festival of One-Act Plays Competition. With that, she was hooked, knowing she had found her place in the theatre. Now, more than twenty-five of her plays have been published by various publishing companies. Her plays have been performed at many theatres including The Gettysburg College, The Globe of the Great Southwest, The American Theatre of Actors and the Paw Paw Village Players. Her plays for teens have enjoyed wide success with many going all the way to national speech and forensics competitions.

Laurie Allen may be contacted at txplaywright@aol.com.

# Order Form

Meriwether Publishing Ltd.
PO Box 7710
Colorado Springs, CO 80933-7710
Phone: 800-937-5297  Fax: 719-594-9916
Website: www.meriwether.com

*Please send me the following books:*

| | | |
|---|---|---|
| _____ | **Comedy Plays and Scenes for Student Actors  #BK-B320**<br>by Laurie Allen<br>*Short sketches for young performers* | **$17.95** |
| _____ | **Comedy Scenes for Student Actors #BK-B308**<br>by Laurie Allen<br>*Short sketches for young performers* | **$17.95** |
| _____ | **Sixty Comedy Duet Scenes for Teens #BK-B302**<br>by Laurie Allen<br>*Real-life situations for laughter* | **$17.95** |
| _____ | **Thirty Short Comedy Plays for Teens #BK-B292**<br>by Laurie Allen<br>*Plays for a variety of cast sizes* | **$16.95** |
| _____ | **Ten-Minute Plays for Middle School Performers  #BK-B305**<br>by Rebecca Young<br>*Plays for a variety of cast sizes* | **$17.95** |
| _____ | **Improv Ideas  #BK-B283**<br>by Justine Jones and Mary Ann Kelley<br>*A book of games and lists* | **$23.95** |
| _____ | **Acting Duets for Young Women #BK-B317**<br>by Laurie Allen<br>*8- to 10-minute duo scenes for practice and competition* | **$17.95** |

**These and other fine Meriwether Publishing books are available at your local bookstore or direct from the publisher. Prices subject to change without notice. Check our website or call for current prices.**

Name: _____ email:_____

Organization name: _____

Address: _____

City: _____ State: _____

Zip: _____ Phone: _____

❑  **Check enclosed**

❑  **Visa / MasterCard / Discover / Am. Express #** _____

*Signature:* _____   Expiration date: _____ / _____
            *(required for credit card orders)*

**Colorado residents:** Please add 3% sales tax.
**Shipping:** Include $3.95 for the first book and 75¢ for each additional book ordered.

❑  *Please send me a copy of your complete catalog of books and plays.*

# Order Form

**Meriwether Publishing Ltd.**
PO Box 7710
Colorado Springs, CO 80933-7710
Phone: 800-937-5297  Fax: 719-594-9916
Website: www.meriwether.com

*Please send me the following books:*

| | | |
|---|---|---|
| _____ | **Comedy Plays and Scenes for Student Actors  #BK-B320**<br>by Laurie Allen<br>*Short sketches for young performers* | $17.95 |
| _____ | **Comedy Scenes for Student Actors #BK-B308**<br>by Laurie Allen<br>*Short sketches for young performers* | $17.95 |
| _____ | **Sixty Comedy Duet Scenes for Teens #BK-B302**<br>by Laurie Allen<br>*Real-life situations for laughter* | $17.95 |
| _____ | **Thirty Short Comedy Plays for Teens #BK-B292**<br>by Laurie Allen<br>*Plays for a variety of cast sizes* | $16.95 |
| _____ | **Ten-Minute Plays for Middle School Performers  #BK-B305**<br>by Rebecca Young<br>*Plays for a variety of cast sizes* | $17.95 |
| _____ | **Improv Ideas  #BK-B283**<br>by Justine Jones and Mary Ann Kelley<br>*A book of games and lists* | $23.95 |
| _____ | **Acting Duets for Young Women #BK-B317**<br>by Laurie Allen<br>*8- to 10-minute duo scenes for practice and competition* | $17.95 |

**These and other fine Meriwether Publishing books are available at your local bookstore or direct from the publisher. Prices subject to change without notice. Check our website or call for current prices.**

Name: _____ email:_____

Organization name: _____

Address: _____

City: _____ State: _____

Zip: _____ Phone: _____

❑  **Check enclosed**

❑  **Visa / MasterCard / Discover / Am. Express #** _____

Signature: _____

*Expiration date:* _____ / _____

*(required for credit card orders)*

**Colorado residents:** Please add 3% sales tax.
**Shipping:** Include $3.95 for the first book and 75¢ for each additional book ordered.

❑  *Please send me a copy of your complete catalog of books and plays.*